COMMUNICATION LAW AND POLICY

Volume 7 Autumn 2002 Number 4

SPECIAL ISSUE

SIEBERT'S SECOND PROPOSITION IN THE TWENTY-FIRST CENTURY: SOCIETY, GOVERNMENT AND FREE EXPRESSION AFTER 9/11

COMMUNICATION LAW AND POLICY

Volume 7 | Autumn 2002 | Number 4

COMMUNICATION LAW AND POLICY

Volume 7 Autumn 2002 Number 4

EDITORIAL NOTE

In 1952, legal scholar and historian Fredrick S. Siebert published his monumental study of three centuries of press freedom in England, in which he enunciated and supported two propositions that were remarkable for their simplicity. The second of the propositions, in particular, has become a guiding principle in the study of free expression.[1] "The area of freedom contracts and the enforcement of restraints increases," Siebert wrote, "as the stresses on the stability of the government and of the structure of society increase."[2]

During the subsequent fifty years, there has been no significant challenge to Siebert's Proposition II. This is not to say that the proposition has not been critiqued or even criticized. Indeed, Professor Siebert himself was taken aback with the attention the proposition received. More than twenty years after he developed the proposition, Professor Siebert said he didn't believe it "was that good."[3] At least one historian agreed. Professor Leonard Levy, himself not unknown to scholarly controversy, told an interviewer in 1980 that the proposition "has practically no validity for American history especially after the framing of the Constitution and the First Amendment."[4] The journalists prosecuted under the Sedition Act of 1798 and the protestors expressing radical sentiments during World War I did not constitute a threat to the stability of society, Levy said. "Siebert was a great scholar and that's a first-class book," he said, "but I don't think that Proposition II should be universalized and made into some timeless truth."[5]

The criticism is by no means universal. Rather than throwing out the proposition as invalid, most scholars have tinkered with it, even

---

[1]Siebert's First Proposition was, "The extent of government control of the press depends on the nature of the relationship of the government to those subject to the government." FREDRICK S. SIEBERT, FREEDOM OF THE PRESS IN ENGLAND 1476–1776: THE RISE AND DECLINE OF GOVERNMENT CONTROL 10 (1952).

[2]*Id.*

[3]Richard A. Schwarzlose, *A Conversation with Fredrick S. Siebert,* 5 JOURNALISM HIST. 106, 108 (1978–79).

[4]Terry Hynes, *A Conversation with Leonard Levy,* 7 JOURNALISM HIST. 96, 102 (1980).

[5]*Id.*

as they recognized its widespread value and potential. "Whether there is sufficient evidence within Siebert's own work to support these propositions can be argued," wrote historian John D. Stevens. "What cannot be disputed is their heuristic value. Since their publication, virtually every study of press freedom has hearkened to them."[6]

Professor Stevens suggested that the word "perceived" might be inserted before the word "stresses" because "in times of peril those involved always overestimate the danger."[7] Professor Stevens also expanded upon Siebert's propositions, suggesting an additional two. "In tribute to his pioneering work," Stevens wrote, "these are numbered from where he stopped." Professor Stevens suggested that a third proposition might be, "The more heterogeneous a society, the more freedom of expression it will tolerate,"[8] and that the fourth might be "the more developed a society, the more subtle will be the controls it exerts on expression."[9]

In the end, however, Professor Stevens praised Siebert's propositions, explaining that his critique, at least in part, was designed to encourage research into the still "untapped potential" of Siebert's Proposition II.[10]

Therein lies the purpose of this special issue of *Communication Law and Policy.*

Few crises in United States history have had the impact of the tragic events of September 11, 2001. As fear and shock turned to outrage, the governors and the governed joined to find answers to what may be unanswerable questions. In an effort to assuage fears while at the same time plotting a course back to normalcy, the governors, often with the approval of the governed, began to inhibit liberties that heretofore had been taken for granted.

Good citizens, who love the United States no less than those reacting aggressively to the terrorist attacks, came under attack themselves for wondering aloud whether civil liberties—including freedom of speech and of the press—deserved more protection and attention than they were getting. These citizens were subjects of threats, abuse and, in some cases, legal actions.

[6]John D. Stevens, *Freedom of Expression: New Dimensions, in* MASS MEDIA AND THE NATIONAL EXPERIENCE 15 (Ronald T. Farrar & John D. Stevens eds., 1971).

[7]*Id.*

[8]*Id.* at 17.

[9]*Id.* at 26

[10]*Id.* at 15.

Stress was impacting the stability of society; the area of freedom of expression was contracting. Indeed, the articles published in this special issue demonstrate the durability of Siebert's Proposition II.[11]

Margaret A. Blanchard, of the University of North Carolina at Chapel Hill and one of the country's leading First Amendment historians, leads off the special issue with an essay examining—even as Siebert did—cycles of stability and stress and the reactions to those cycles. In an essay challenging First Amendment scholars to continue to explore these issues, she proposes that society goes through cycles that she labels "repressive" and "reactive."[12] After surveying some three centuries of free speech in the United States, she proposes, with her usual eloquence and power, that we learn from the cycles and, in times of stress, we advocate more discussion, debate and criticism.

Susan Dente Ross, of Washington State University, goes one step further. Also recognizing the tendency to restrict radical dissent during times of stress, Professor Ross proposes a test to protect such speech. She asserts that radical dissent, rather than harming society, is, in fact, beneficial to self-government and the search for truth.[13] The Supreme Court, therefore, should adopt a five-part test to protect such speech.[14]

Kathleen Olson, of Lehigh University, applies a concept developed by scholar Vincent Blasi—the pathological perspective[15]—to courtroom access issues following September 11. The pathological perspective takes as its starting point the view that it is almost always beneficial to have judicial proceedings open to the public and the press, and that, therefore, all such proceedings are presumptively open. This change would take away the ability of judges to engage in ad hoc decision making and would bring about a higher level of certainty regarding courtroom access.[16] Judicial proceedings would only

---

[11]Special thanks go to the following members of the journal's editorial board who made special efforts to review the articles submitted for this issue under the considerable stress of deadline pressure: Patricia Aufderheide, Timothy Brennan, Matthew Bunker, Everette Dennis, Robert Drechsel, Timothy Gleason, Kermit Hall, Steven Helle, Jeremy Lipschultz, Gregory Lisby, Robert O'Neil, Todd Simon, Rodney Smolla, Dwight Teeter and Ruth Walden.

[12]Margaret A. Blanchard, *"Why Can't We Ever Learn?" Cycles of Stability, Stress and Freedom of Expression in United States History,* 7 COMM. L. & POL'Y 347, 349 (2002).

[13]Susan Dente Ross, *An Apologia to Radical Dissent and a Supreme Court Test to Protect It,* 7 COMM. L. & POL'Y 401, 404 (2002).

[14]*Id.* at 427–28.

[15]*See* Vincent Blasi, *The Pathological Perspective and the First Amendment,* 85 COLUM. L. REV. 449, 456–57 (1985).

[16]Kathleen K. Olson, *Courtroom Access After 9/11: A Pathological Perspective,* 7 COMM. L. & POL'Y 461, 494 (2002).

be closed if the government could meet the two-pronged strict scrutiny test.[17] It beats the *Richmond Newspapers* two-part test, she writes.[18]

Kenton Bird and Elizabeth Brandt of the University of Idaho, also take on a highly specific topic. They provide a chilling account of how times of stress—the period following the events of September 11, in particular—inhibit academic freedom.[19] Unfortunately, they provide little hope for the future—an implicit call for additional study in this vital area of free expression.

Jeffery Smith's article provides an overview of Fredrick Siebert's life and work.[20] Smith, from the University of Wisconsin–Milwaukee, examined Siebert's papers and those of the Association for Education in Journalism and Mass Communication, along with other historical sources, in an attempt to construct a foundation from which to examine the philosophical and legal underpinnings of the Second Proposition. His article provides a fresh new approach to the context in which Siebert developed his propositions and the significance they continue to hold.

In all, this special issue provides a remarkable body of work focusing on one of legal history's key propositions in the context of one of today's great tragedies.

—W. Wat Hopkins

[17]*Id.* at 492–93.

[18]*Id.*

[19]R. Kenton Bird & Elizabeth Barker Brandt, *Academic Freedom and 9/11: How the War on Terrorism Threatens Free Speech on Campus,* 7 COMM. L. & POL'Y 431, (2002).

[20]Jeffery A. Smith, *Fredrick Siebert's Absolute, Adjustable First Amendment,* 7 COMM. L. & POL'Y 379 (2002).

7 COMM. L. & POL'Y 347–378 (2002)

"WHY CAN'T WE EVER LEARN?" CYCLES OF STABILITY, STRESS AND FREEDOM OF EXPRESSION IN UNITED STATES HISTORY

MARGARET A. BLANCHARD*

Freedom of expression in the United States may well run in two almost parallel cycles. History shows that repressive cycles, which Fredrick Seaton Siebert discussed, are generally followed by reactive cycles in which freedom of expression expands. The question of how these cycles develop and relate to one another is discussed in the essay below. Also examined is the question of why the periods of repression of expression are better remembered than the times when freedom of expression expanded. The basic issue involved is best summarized in the question: "Why can't we ever learn?"

The student looked perplexed as she raised her hand. We were deep into our discussion of the effect of the Cold War on freedom of expression in the United States. "Didn't we just do that in World War I?" she asked, referring to the litany of legislation enacted to suppress dissent. The legislation had not worked very well in World War I; dissent continued as dissenters went to jail. "Why can't we ever learn," she asked, that dissent does not harm the country?

As a scholar, Frederick S. Seibert apparently took such repetition of efforts at repression in stride. He even developed a proposition to state the situation as a scientist would: "The area of freedom contracts and the enforcement of restraints increases as the stresses on the stability of the government and of the structure of society increase."[1] Seibert was talking about the British experience, for his

---

*William Rand Kenan Jr. Professor of Journalism and Mass Communication, University of North Carolina at Chapel Hill.

[1]FREDRICK SEATON SIEBERT, FREEDOM OF THE PRESS IN ENGLAND 1476–1776: THE RISE AND DECLINE OF GOVERNMENT CONTROL 10 (1965).

propositions evolved from his landmark study of the history of freedom of expression in England. My student put the situation far more simply and based her assessment on a semester's worth of study of the history of freedom of expression in the United States.

Her question—"why can't we ever learn?"—neatly and precisely encapsulates the American experience with freedom of expression. Crisis after crisis, the same set of problems related to expression arise only to disappear after the nation successfully navigates the danger. Repressive activities reappear with a degree of predictability that is frightening when the next crisis appears on the horizon. Perhaps, then, there are cycles to freedom of expression—cycles that do not quite repeat themselves precisely, but cycles that repeat themselves sufficiently to make their study worthwhile.

Historians have explored the notion of cycles in history, although not in context of freedom of expression.[2] The exploration has often focused on that illusive effort to prove that although history does not repeat itself exactly, it does follow certain patterns over time. Knowledge of such patterns may lead to predictive abilities and fuller appreciation of how events develop and interact. In each examination, the notion is clear that there are striking similarities between events in American history, although the precise repetition of events does not occur. Given this understanding, the period of stress following the events of September 11, 2001, which is the focus of the articles in this special edition, might well benefit from a review of the history related to freedom of expression that it and the people in it are emulating.

If time periods are examined carefully, the most important similarity in terms of cycles of freedom of speech seems to be the belief that American society will be destroyed if restrictions on freedom of expression are not implemented. Information must be controlled; speech must be limited; criticism of government actions must be eliminated. National security is the byword, and the enemy may be external as in the terrorist attacks on the World Trade Center buildings on September 11, or internal as in the actions that led to the round-up and continued incarceration of people of Arab descent following the attacks. Most cycles of restricted freedom of expression combine both external and internal dangers, a fact that makes the government and its people even more apprehensive. The vital goal in

[2]ARTHUR M. SCHLESINGER, PATHS TO THE PRESENT (1949); ARTHUR M. SCHLESINGER, JR., THE CYCLES OF AMERICAN HISTORY (1986); Frank L. Klingberg, *Cyclical Trends in American Foreign Policy Moods and Their Policy Implications*, *in* CHALLENGES TO AMERICA: U.S. FOREIGN POLICY IN THE 1980S 89 (C.W. Kegley, Jr., & P.J. McGowan eds., 1979).

such a time period, as Seibert discovered, is the preservation of the nation. For, as advocates of swift and stern government action against dissent in such time periods successfully argue, without the government, there would be no rights. Consequently, they say, it makes sense to preserve the government at the expense of momentary restrictions on civil liberties, including the right of freedom of expression.

Such debate hovers in the halls of Congress today and often dominates statements made by executive branch spokesmen. In light of terrorist threats, the argument goes, civil liberties—such as privacy of electronic communication and the right to disagree with the government—must give way to the much more substantial need to protect the government. And protecting the government essentially means allowing only speech that agrees with the government stance. Such comments reverberate through the history of the United States and reveal just how fragile the right to freedom of expression is. Such is the first cycle of the history of freedom of expression.

Lagging a bit behind this cycle of repression is a cycle of reaction to suppression that does indeed show the importance of freedom of speech. This second cycle, which may be termed a reactive cycle, exists even during the repressive cycle, but it is much less apparent early in the repressive event. Slowly, adherents of free speech make headway in the halls of Congress and the national psyche. Eventually the concern about freedom of expression reaches the general populace, and the demand for the right to disagree with the government increases. Slowly, the nation and its people right themselves and reassert the importance of the fundamental rights on which the nation was founded and has existed for more than two centuries.

This cycle of reaction to suppression of dissent seems even more misunderstood than the cycle of repression that Siebert and others have written about so profoundly. We can all name the repressive incidents: the events preceding the John Peter Zenger trial, the Stamp Act, the Alien and Sedition Acts, the suppression of the Copperhead press in the Civil War, the repressive legislation that dominated World War I and the witch-hunts of the McCarthy period. We do an excellent job teaching these events in order to encourage our students, our colleagues and ourselves to remain ever vigilant in the face of challenges to freedom of expression. As my student said: "Why can't we ever learn?"

Recent history, however, has shown that there is still another level where, as a nation and as supporters of free speech, we have problems learning and that rests in the cycle of reaction to suppression. This cycle picks up slowly but surely; in the midst of every crisis it brings progress in the area of free speech. The progress is often ignored. In the days immediately after September 11, many of my colleagues went around quoting Justice Oliver Wendell Holmes in *Schenck v. United States*[3] to the effect that certain freedoms—including those of free expression—must be sacrificed in time of war. This interpretation ignores the eighty-some years that have passed since this first case interpreting the First Amendment was handed down. Things have changed. World War II and the Vietnam War experience left a lasting legacy of freedom of speech—a legacy that was built on events that developed over the nation's history.

The purpose of this essay is to introduce the idea that cycles of freedom of expression may well exist in American history. Further, this research proposes to look into the possibility that two cycles have developed over time: a repressive cycle that limits freedom of expression and a reactive cycle that works to restore the importance of freedom of expression in American society. Slightly more emphasis will be given to the reactive cycle because it is that cycle that we as Americans seem to know the least about. This is an exploratory study designed to examine the possibilities of such cycles, not the final word on the topic. The possibilities the study of these cycles offer, however, could well be instructive.

THE EIGHTEENTH-CENTURY EXPERIENCE

The repressive cycle extends far back in our history. We could, for instance, begin our study with the John Peter Zenger trial, which helped to secure the right of citizens in the colonies to criticize their rulers.[4] Or, we could start with the Stamp Act crisis, which taught the colonists the importance of being able to print without special taxation on their products.[5]

---

[3]249 U.S. 47 (1919).

[4]*See* JAMES ALEXANDER, A BRIEF NARRATIVE OF THE CASE AND TRIAL OF JOHN PETER ZENGER, PRINTER OF THE NEW YORK WEEKLY JOURNAL (Stanley Nider Katz ed., 1963) (1736); LIVINGSTON RUTHERFORD, JOHN PETER ZENGER: HIS PRESS, HIS TRIAL, AND A BIBLIOGRAPHY OF ZENGER IMPRINTS (1904); Cathy Covert, *"Passion Is Ye Prevailing Motive": The Feud Behind the Zenger Case*, 50 JOURNALISM Q. 3, 3–10 (1973); David Paul Nord, *The Authority of Truth: Religion and the John Peter Zenger Case*, 62 JOURNALISM Q. 227, 227–35 (1985); Warren C. Price, *Reflections on the Trial of John Peter Zenger*, 32 JOURNALISM Q. 161, 161–68 (1955).

[5]*See* EDMUND S. MORGAN & HELEN M. MORGAN, THE STAMP ACT CRISIS, PROLOGUE TO REVOLUTION (2d ed. 1995); ARTHUR M. SCHLESINGER, PRELUDE TO INDEPENDENCE: THE NEWSPAPER WAR ON BRITAIN, 1764–1776 (1958).

We will, however, begin with the first well-documented example: the Alien and Sedition Acts of 1798.[6] President John Adams feared a possible war with France. He also feared losing the presidency to Thomas Jefferson in 1800, and Jefferson supported France. Consequently the two evils merged in the psyches of Adams and his followers. Protecting the country from France very clearly meant protecting the country from Jefferson and his followers.

"[E]very independent Government has a right to preserve and defend itself against injuries and outrages which endanger its existence,"[7] argued Harrison Gray Otis, Federalist from Massachusetts. Criticism of the government obviously was dangerous, especially in time of international peril. Freedom of speech or of the press surely could not be interpreted to mean freedom to speak against the nation's leaders or policies in such a situation. "[I]t is clearly understood," Otis continued, "that to punish licentiousness and sedition is not a restraint or abridgement of freedom of speech or of the press."[8]

Federalist John Allen of Connecticut had similar feelings and was far more specific about his concerns. "Because the Constitution guaranties [sic] ... freedom of the press, am I at liberty to falsely call you a thief, a murder, an atheist?" Never, he claimed. "The freedom of the press and opinions was never understood to give the right of publishing falsehoods and slanders, nor of exciting sedition, insurrection, and slaughter, with impunity."[9] These two quotes, brief though they are, show the qualities of repressive cycles of history. The nation is threatened—clearly or not—by a combination of internal and external forces. Government leaders and their supporters desire to protect the government at all costs. It is not reasonable, as Otis said, to allow a threat to imperil the nation's very existence. To fellow Federalist Robert Goodloe Harper of South Carolina, the problem was Blackstonian[10] in nature. Liberty of the press simply meant "every man might publish what he pleased; but if he abused this liberty so as to publish slanders against his neighbor, or false,

---

[6]*See* JOHN C. MILLER, CRISIS IN FREEDOM: THE ALIEN AND SEDITION ACTS (1951); JAMES MORTON SMITH, FREEDOM'S FETTERS: THE ALIEN AND SEDITION LAWS AND AMERICAN CIVIL LIBERTIES (1956).

[7]2 ANNALS OF CONG. 2146 (1798);

[8]*Id.* at 2148–49.

[9]*Id.* at 2097.

[10]Leaders of the new nation were greatly influenced by William Blackstone's writings on prior restraint. Blackstone condemned previous restraints, but he had no problems with post-publication reaction to publication. 4 WILLIAM BLACKSTONE, COMMENTARIES ON THE LAWS OF ENGLAND 151–52 (T.B. Wait and Sons 1818).

scandalous, and malicious libels against the magistrates, or the Government, he became liable to punishment."[11]

Responsible citizens simply would not criticize government in times of peril; they would know the importance of allowing the government to carry out its plans without interference from the citizenry who could not know the dangers facing the nation. All the Sedition Act did was draw a line around freedom of expression. Speech inside the circle was permissible; speech outside the circle was not. Federalist speech was inside the circle; Republican speech was outside. The problem in John Adams' day was very simple, much as it has been in the last two hundred years. Times of crisis demand responsible speech; good citizens honored that demand and helped to preserve the nation.

Interestingly, though, Adams' opponents in the Republican Party agreed with the president in the essential idea of protecting the government from criticism in time of trouble. The Republicans wanted to punish speech that criticized the president just as much as the Federalists did. They just wanted to change the venue for considering whether the speech constituted a danger to the nation. Federalists wanted trials held in federal courts; Jefferson's supporters favored state court jurisdiction. Federalists controlled the federal courts; Republicans had leverage on the state court level. Political repression was clearly coupled with national security, and separating the two seemed almost impossible. The only question that remained was *where* national security should be protected.

After Congress approved the legislation and Adams signed it into law, Jefferson and his colleague James Madison, father of the Constitution, continued the battle for the minds of men. The two combined to author—anonymously—the Virginia and Kentucky Resolutions.[12] Jefferson's language in the Kentucky resolution reflected his ambivalence about freedom of expression. The constitutional language, he said, meant that the people of the states intended to "retain to themselves the right of judging how far the licentiousness of speech and of the press may be abridged without lessening their useful freedom, and how far those abuses which cannot be separated from their use should be tolerated."[13] Here Jefferson showed his belief in restric-

[11]2 ANNALS OF CONG. 2167–68 (1798).

[12]Adrienne Koch & Harry Ammon, *The Virginia and Kentucky Resolutions: An Episode in Jefferson's and Madison's Defense of Civil Liberties*, 5 (3d ser.) WM. & MARY Q. 145, 145–76 (1948).

[13]Thomas Jefferson, *Resolutions Relative to the Alien and Sedition Laws*, *in* THE WRITINGS OF THOMAS JEFFERSON 381 (Albert Ellery Bergh ed., 1907).

tions on freedom of expression that showed its licentious nature. If we had only Jefferson's words to rely on, we would not make much progress beyond the repressive cycle inaugurated by John Adams with the Sedition Act.

James Madison, on the other hand, expanded the concept of freedom of expression substantially. In his Virginia resolutions, he stressed that "some degree of abuse is inseparable from the proper use of every thing, and in no instance is this more true than in that of the press."[14] Thus, the states had decided "that it is better to leave a few of its noxious branches to their luxuriant growth, than, by pruning them away, to injure the vigour of those yielding proper fruits." The wisdom of such a practice was obvious, said Madison, who proclaimed to "the press alone, chequered as it is with abuses, the world is indebted for all the triumphs which have improved their political system into a shape so auspicious to their happiness." He asked:

> [If] forbidding every publication that might bring the constituted agents into contempt or disrepute, or that might excite the hatred of the people against the authors of unjust or pernicious, [had] been uniformly enforced against the press, might not the United States have been languishing at this day under the infirmities of a sickly Confederation?[15]

Further, he questioned, "Might they not, possibly, be miserable colonies, groaning under a foreign yoke?[16]

Beyond the connection between free expression and the freedom of the colonies, Madison saw even further issues related to freedom of the press. In commentary that separated him from many of his contemporaries, Madison voiced his disapproval of post-publication retribution for misdeeds of the press. Blackstone's formulation of freedom of the press, he wrote:

> [C]an never be admitted to the American idea of it; since a law inflicting penalties on printed publications would have a similar effect with a law authorizing a previous restraint on them. It would seem a mockery to say that no laws should be passed preventing publications from being

[14]James Madison, *Report on the Resolutions, 1799–1800, in* 6 THE WRITINGS OF JAMES MADISON 389 (Galliard Hunt ed., 1906).

[15]*Id.* at 386.

[16]*Id.*

made, but that laws might be passed for punishing them in case they should be made.[17]

This comes close to saying that no law can be put into effect punishing the press for material printed because the fear of post-publication legal action is as chilling to free expression as prior restraint.

Few remember these statements by Madison, and little was done to build a structure of freedom of expression on them. These statements clearly were part of the reaction to the repressive activities of the Alien and Sedition Act period. Yet the opening for expansion of the right of freedom of expression was somehow lost in the stories of Republican editors jailed for their criticisms of Adams and his administration. The question here is why has the emphasis been on the negative rather than on the positive? Why was this opening for expanding protection for the press not exploited? Why are the Virginia and Kentucky Resolutions remembered more for their contribution to state's rights and nullification than for their contribution to freedom of expression? Why can't we ever learn?

THE NINETEENTH-CENTURY EXPERIENCE

The nineteenth-century experience with freedom of expression is also dismal. The focus is often on the Civil War and the limitations placed on freedom of expression. Lincoln is remembered for suspending the writ of habeas corpus[18] and for closing down New York City newspapers after they published a false call for a day of prayer and public humiliation because of Union losses.[19] The Union imposed censorship during the Civil War[20] and Congress enacted a seditious conspiracy law,[21] although it was not enforced. That is enough re-

[17]*Id.*

[18]*See* HAROLD M. HYMAN, A MORE PERFECT UNION: THE IMPACT OF THE CIVIL WAR AND RECONSTRUCTION ON THE CONSTITUTION 81–98 (1973); JAMES G. RANDALL, CONSTITUTIONAL PROBLEMS UNDER LINCOLN (rev. ed. 1951); DEAN SPRAGUE, FREEDOM UNDER LINCOLN (1965); Sherrill Halbert, *The Suspension of the Writ of Habeas Corpus by President Lincoln*, 2 AM. J. OF LEGAL HIST. 95, 95–115 (1958).

[19]RANDALL, *supra* note 18, at 496–97

[20]*See* J. CUTLER ANDREWS, THE NORTH REPORTS THE CIVIL WAR (1955); JOSEPH J. MATHEWS, REPORTING THE WARS (1957); Adolph O. Goldsmith, *Reporting the Civil War: Union Army Press Relations*, 33 JOURNALISM Q. 478, 478–87 (1956); James G. Randall, *The Newspaper Problem in Its Bearing Upon Military Secrecy During the Civil War*, 23 AM. HIST. REV. 303, 303–23 (1918).

[21]The provisions of the law made it a crime if two or more persons conspired to overthrow the government of the United States, to levy war against the United States or to impede the execution of the laws of the United States. Conspiracy Act of 1861, ch. 33, § 12, Stat. 284 (1861) (current version at 42 U.S.C. S 1985(2) (1994)).

pression of free speech to convince anyone that the United States was in another repressive cycle. The internal and external security of the country clearly was at risk during these years, and the government once again acted to preserve its very existence.

The reactive response to this incursion on freedom of expression came from the United States Supreme Court, although its actions have not made their way into the traditional annals of the history of free speech. The Court, in fact, heard five cases based on speech-related activities, one of which more or less upheld the conviction. The latter case involved Clement L. Vallandigham, an Ohio politician who was a Democratic member of Congress.[22] Vallandigham argued steadfastly against the war, criticizing the way in which the draft was skewed against poor men who could not pay the $300 necessary to avoid service and urging that the fighting cease immediately with northern troops abandoning southern territory. Vallandigham assumed the leadership of the peace movement in the Midwest, and while his conviction for speaking against the war was being appealed, Lincoln sent Vallandigham behind the Confederate lines.

The Court heard Vallandigham's case,[23] which was based on his criticism of the war, on the right of a military court to try a civilian in wartime. Although Vallandigham would argue publicly that he was facing conviction based on his political opinion, the Supreme Court refused to review his case because, the justices explained, their jurisdiction did not extend to the review of decisions handed down by military courts.[24] The justices were clearly skirting the issue because they did not want to interfere with military justice while men still fought and died on the battlefield. Even so, the very fact that a politician would publicly oppose the Civil War is an important development in the history of freedom of expression—an important stage in the reactive cycle to the suppression of that war.

Vallandigham was not alone in his dissent. Lambdin P. Milligan, an Indiana businessman, gave voice to his views against the war as well.[25] Milligan, as with Vallandigham, believed that the Midwest

The crime was one step away from treason and focused primarily on the planning and discussion of such activities. *See* Catherine M. Tarrant, *To "Insure Domestic Tranquility": Congress and the Law of Seditious Conspiracy, 1859–1861*, 15 AM. J. OF LEGAL HIST. 107, 107–23 (1971).

[22]*See* FRANK L. KLEMENT, THE LIMITS OF DISSENT: CLEMENT L. VALLANDIGHAM & THE CIVIL WAR (1970).

[23]Ex parte Vallandigham, 68 U.S. 243 (1864).

[24]*Id.*

[25]*See* Frank L. Klement, *The Indianapolis Treason Trials and* Ex Parte Milligan, *in* AMERICAN POLITICAL TRIALS 101–27 (Michal R. Belknap ed., 1981); Allan Nevins, *The Case of the Copperhead Conspirator*, *in* QUARRELS THAT HAVE SHAPED THE

could only suffer gravely as a result of the war. His opposition differed from Vallandigham's, however, because he became tied up in a secret society of southerners opposed to the war. Even though he was not philosophically connected with a "dark lantern society," Milligan and others were arrested and charged with conspiring against the United States government, providing aid and comfort to the Confederates, participating in disloyal practices, and violating the laws of war. Following a ten-week trial on treason charges before a military court, Milligan and three others were found guilty. Three of the defendants, including Milligan, were sentenced to death; the fourth was sentenced to hard labor for the duration of the war. President Andrew Johnson commuted the sentences to life imprisonment.

Milligan's case reached the Supreme Court after the fighting had stopped.[26] Faced with a situation much the same as that involved in Vallandigham's case—trial by military tribunal in a free state—the Court this time ruled that as long as civilian courts were operating, civilians must be tried there rather than in military courts. At this point, there had been no discussion of possible meaning for the First Amendment in the Supreme Court or elsewhere, and the Court felt that the time was not right to begin such an interpretation. The supremacy of civilian courts was the important issue to address. But Milligan's case was another contribution to the reaction cycle to the repression of the Civil War.

The Court made further gains on the Radical Republicans' plan for Reconstruction when it considered cases involving the Ironclad Oath.[27] The Radical Republicans, determined that no former Confederates would be allowed to retake positions of authority in the re-united Union, enacted the Ironclad Oath in 1862.[28] The oath was to past, present and future allegiance to the Union. No one who had voluntarily participated in the rebellion or had aided it in any way or who had held office under the Confederacy could qualify for federal jobs at the end of the war. Lincoln favored only an oath of future allegiance, but the Radicals won out. Many state courts adopted the Ironclad Oath as well. The Supreme Court cases involved a state oath and the federal oath.

CONSTITUTION 90–108 (John A. Garraty ed., 1962); Kenneth M. Stampp, *The Milligan Case and the Election of 1864 in Indiana*, 31 MISSISSIPPI VALLEY HIST. REV. 41, 41–58 (1944).

[26]Ex parte Milligan, 71 U.S. 2 (1866).

[27]*See* HAROLD MELVIN HYMAN, ERA OF THE OATH: NORTHERN LOYALTY TESTS DURING THE CIVIL WAR AND RECONSTRUCTION (1954).

[28]12 Stat. 502 (1862).

The state oath case addressed a revision of the Missouri constitution in 1865 that required an oath of past loyalty from a variety of persons including members of the clergy. John Cummings, a Roman Catholic priest, refused to take the oath, based largely on the grounds that the requirement violated his religious freedom. Cummings continued to work and teach among the people of Missouri without the required license and was arrested, tried, convicted, imprisoned and fined $500. Part of Cummings' difficulty with the oath was its imputation that he had never done anything that could have been considered hostile to the state government. Missouri was a border state that was rife with conflict during the Civil War; ascertaining the political beliefs of those he was aiding seemed untenable at best under such circumstances. State officials refused to consider the constitutional provision as a violation of religious freedom, an *ex post facto* law,[29] or a bill of attainder.[30]

By a 5–4 majority, the Supreme Court refused to accept the state's arguments, ruling that the state provision established legislative punishments for actions performed before the document was even written. The oath was unconstitutional on both *ex post facto* and bill of attainder grounds. Justice Stephen Field, writing for the majority, condemned the Missouri oath "for its severity, without any precedent that we can discover."[31] Not only was the time period covered unacceptable, but "the oath is directed not merely against overt and visible acts of hostility to the government, but is intended to reach words, desires, and sympathies, also." In addition, the oath "allows no distinction between acts springing from malignant enmity and acts which might have been prompted by charity, or affection, or relationship."[32]

The second test oath case, decided the same day, involved the Ironclad Oath enacted by the U.S. Congress and focused on a lawyer from Arkansas who wanted to resume his practice before the Supreme Court. Augustus H. Garland served in both the Confederate House and Senate, but with the end of the war, he received a presidential pardon and petitioned to resume his practice before the Supreme Court despite the ironclad loyalty oath that barred former Confederate of-

[29]An *ex post facto* law is a punishment after the offense is committed. It is unconstitutional because individuals must be aware that they are committing a crime at the time of the action.

[30]A bill of attainder is a legislative act declaring certain individuals guilty of crimes without trials. They are unconstitutional because the legislature may not declare persons guilty of crimes without allowing them to stand trial and defend themselves.

[31]Cummings v. Missouri, 71 U.S. 277, 318 (1867).

[32]*Id.*

ficeholders. The Court was called upon to interpret the extent of presidential pardoning power.[33] By the same 5–4 margin, the Court found that test oath unconstitutional as applied to lawyers and said that attorneys seeking to practice before it did not have to take the oath. Once the Court admitted an attorney to practice, that individual could be removed only for cause and only by action of the Court itself. In addition, the presidential pardon had erased Garland's guilt.

This would seem to be a three-out-of-four margin for those seeking to end the repression of the Civil War era, and indeed it was. Radical Republicans, however, were unhappy because the Court majorities had been comprised of individuals who had achieved their places on the Supreme Court before Lincoln had begun to name his justices. The decisions, argued the Radicals, were coming from pro-southern justices and should not be allowed to stand. Consequently Congress stanched the reactive cycle and fortified its opponents.

The last free speech case involved Colonel William H. McCardle, a former Confederate officer who was editor of the *Vicksburg Times* in Mississippi.[34] McCardle used the pages of his newspaper to stymie as many Radical Republican Reconstruction plans as possible. Eventually he was arrested for using his newspaper to disturb the peace; incite insurrection, disorder and violence; libel Union General E. O. C. Ord; and impede Reconstruction by keeping voters away from the polls. Military authorities had McCardle in custody for almost two weeks before bringing him before a military commission to answer for his crimes. When arraigned, McCardle refused to enter a plea, contending that his attorneys were seeking his release on a writ of habeas corpus in the federal court system. Using the Milligan doctrine, he argued that the military had no right to try him, a civilian.

McCardle lost his appeal in lower courts, and his attorneys pursued the matter into the Supreme Court. McCardle's attorneys wanted to use his case to end the Reconstruction process. The Su-

---

[33]Ex parte Garland, 71 U.S. 333 (1867). Congress got around the Court's disapproval of the Ironclad Oath by writing the third section of the Fourteenth Amendment, which was ratified in 1868. That language barred any person from federal and state office who "having previously taken an oath, as a member of Congress, or as an officer of the United States, or as a member of any State legislature, or as an executive office of any State, to support the Constitution of the United States, shall have engaged in insurrection or rebellion against the same, or given aid or comfort to the enemies thereof." Congress could remove the disability by a two-thirds vote. U.S. CONST. amend. XIV, § 3.

[34]Sever L. Eubank, *The McCardle Case: A Challenge to Radical Reconstruction*, 18 J. OF MISSISSIPPI HIST. 111, 111–27 (1956); Stanley I. Kutler, Ex parte McCardle: *Judicial Impotence? The Supreme Court and Reconstruction Reconsidered*, 72 AM. HIST. REV. 835, 835–51 (1967).

preme Court aroused congressional concerns by speeding up the process by which it planned to hear the case and by allowing extra time for arguments, actions that stressed the importance attached to the case. Written and oral arguments before the Court focused on the right to trial by jury and on the right of Congress to restructure former rebel states without judicial interference.

Despite the fact that the freedom of the press issue was virtually ignored in the case, one of the written briefs filed on McCardle's behalf raised the issue. "The Constitution declares the Congress shall make no law 'abridging the freedom of speech or of the press,'" the brief declared.[35] "What is the case before the Court? A citizen, not connected with the army or navy, was arrested and imprisoned by a military officer, not for any crime known to any law, but because he published certain articles which criticised [sic] severely the acts of that military commander." General Ord, the brief continued, "established a censorship of the press—nay more; he asserted and exercised a right which is totally destructive of the liberty of the press. ... These [reconstruction] acts authorize all this."[36] The free expression issue was not pursued before the Supreme Court.

Members of the Court began considering the case March 9, 1868, amid Senate preparations to try Andrew Johnson on impeachment charges brought by the House. That same month, Congress passed legislation over the president's veto that repealed the Court's jurisdiction in certain habeas corpus cases. In light of this action, the justices heard arguments again in March 1869 about whether a congressional action could affect a pending case. In April 1869, the Court held that Congress had the right to change its jurisdiction and that those changes could affect a pending case.[37] Even though the Court would not intervene to save McCardle, the government dropped the case. His opposition had become inconsequential.

Here, then, the Supreme Court leaves its first legacy in the cycles of freedom of expression. Caught in the cycle of repression generated by the Civil War, the majority of the justices opted instead to put a stop to some of the examples of egregious revenge being practiced by the northern victors. They created instead the beginnings of a judicial safety net to stop such repression. The reactive cycle that these decisions helped create is clothed in defining and protecting other consti-

---

[35]Brief for the Appellant, Ex parte McCardle, 73 U.S. 318 (1867), *quoted in* 6 (pt. 1) CHARLES FAIRMAN, RECONSTRUCTION AND REUNION 458 (1971).

[36]*Id.*

[37]Ex parte McCardle, 74 U.S. 506 (1869). The Supreme Court later reaffirmed that Reconstruction was a political issue that the legal system should leave alone. *See* Texas v. White, 74 U.S. 700 (1869).

tutional rights—ex post facto laws, bills of attainder, and presidential pardons—but the issues are certainly those involving freedom of expression. Later courts would certainly treat them in that light. Perhaps, then, we have something to learn from this time period.

THE TWENTIETH CENTURY EXPERIENCE: THE EARLY YEARS

World War I is considered one of the most repressive periods in American history. The three branches of the federal government acted to ensure that executive policy, legislation and judicial decisions would combine to silence disagreement with the wartime policies of Woodrow Wilson.[38] As Wilson said to the country on Flag Day 1917, "Woe be to the man or group of men that seeks to stand in our way in this day of high resolution when every principle we hold dearest is to be vindicated and made secure for the salvation of nations."[39] If the people did not have good enough sense to support the country on their own, an armory of legislation stood ready to enforce support. These measures included the Threats Against the President Act,[40] the Espionage Act,[41] the Trading with the Enemy Act,[42] the Sedition Act[43] and the Alien Act.[44]

---

[38]*See* DONALD JOHNSON, THE CHALLENGE TO AMERICAN FREEDOM: WORLD WAR I AND THE RISE OF THE AMERICAN CIVIL LIBERTIES UNION (1963); PAUL L. MURPHY, WORLD WAR I AND THE ORIGIN OF CIVIL LIBERTIES IN THE UNITED STATES (1979); H.C. PETERSON & GILBERT C. FITE, OPPONENTS OF WAR, 1917–1919 (1957); HARRY N. SCHEIBER, THE WILSON ADMINISTRATION AND CIVIL LIBERTIES (1960).

[39]*Flag Day Address* (June 14, 1917), *in* 42 THE PAPERS OF WOODROW WILSON 504 (Arthur S. Link ed., 1983).

[40]H.R. 15314, 65th Cong. (1917) (current version at 18 U.S.C. § 871 (1982)). This was designed to protect the physical person of the president from threats to his life.

[41]H.R. 291, 65th Cong. (1917) (amended, ch. 75, § 1, 40 Stat. 553, 1918) (repealed and original reenacted ch. 136, 41 Stat. 1359, 1921) (repealed ch. 645, § 21, 62 Stat. 862 (1948)). This was aimed primarily at those who spied against the United States. It contained language, however, that punished speech that attempted to disrupt the functioning of the armed services. It also gave the Postmaster General the power to declare nonmailable any material designed to violate any provisions of the act.

[42]H.R. 4960, 65th Cong. (1917) (classified to 50 U.S.C. § 1–6, § 7–39, § 41–44 (1933)). This increased the postmaster general's power by requiring anyone who printed material in a foreign language that dealt with the war to submit a certified English-language version of the work before it could be entered into the mail.

[43]H.R. 8753, 65th Cong. (1918) (repealed ch. 136, 41 Stat. 1359 (1921)). These amendments to the Espionage Act were designed to punish those who used abusive language against the government and its military forces.

[44]H.R. 12402, 65th Cong. (1918) (amended ch. 251, 41 Stat. 1008 (1920)) (current version at 8 U.S.C. § 1424 (2001)). This law was designed to make it easier to deport aliens who were found to have ties to the Communist Party. Previous legislation had included a time limit after which an alien would no longer be at risk for deportation. This law carried no such restrictions.

Although most members of the federal government believed the legislation absolutely essential, some members of Congress opposed parts of it. Senator William E. Borah, Republican of Idaho, for example, argued, "I think one of the greatest services we can render the cause of democracy just now is to demonstrate to the world that a Republic can carry on war, defend itself effectively and triumphantly without recurring to the practices and procedures of absolute governments."[45] One of the "saddest features of his war," he continued:

> [H]as been the haste with which the freer, more liberal governments have adopted the arbitrary and dictatorial policies and practices of the most absolute of governments. There are no democracies at this hour in this conflict, whatever may be the outward form or whatever the fact was before the war, and whatever the fact may be after the war.[46]

If the danger to the United States became greater, Borah was sure that individual citizens would "measure up to the occasion. I at least want to try out this situation to the end and see if a Republic may not be a Republic in war as well as a Republic at peace."[47]

The concern about the nation's ability to maintain its standards despite facing a world war crossed the aisle as well. Senator Charles S. Thomas, Democrat of Colorado, said he believed that, "It is only in time of war that these great constitutional limitations upon despotism are put to the test." Only in wartime do they "become effective and their value is priceless. Consequently, it is at such times that must see to it that they are preserved, lest when peace does return we shall realize that some of the most important safeguards of liberty have been swept away in the torrent of the conflict."[48]

Could Borah be a representative of a reactive cycle beginning about the same time as a repressive cycle? Despite the coincidence in timing and Borah's clear position on the need for freedom of expression, the repressive cycle had a clear edge during this time period. The nation had never been involved in a full-scale war such as this one, and those who were worried about its capacity to survive outnumbered and out-powered those willing to give Americans a chance to show their loyalty and love of their country. It was much better in 1917 and 1918 to have legislation provide the muscle for requests for good behavior by citizens.

---

[45] 54 CONG. REC. 837 (1917).
[46] *Id.*
[47] *Id.*
[48] *Id.* at 789–90.

The Supreme Court proved that it was clearly among the institutions concerned with the behavior of citizens. In *Schenck v. United States*,[49] the case that launched the Court's relationship with the First Amendment, the unanimous justices noted that "[w]hen a nation is at war many things that might be said in time of peace are such a hindrance to its effort that their utterance will not be endured so long as men fight and that no Court could regard them as protected by any constitutional right."[50] This is the quote that some of my colleagues use to tell students that some restrictions on free speech in wartime may well be necessary. This is not, however, the last word on the topic, because the latest word, as we shall see, is much more reactive than it is repressive.

Before the Court could react to many other cases stemming from World War I, another repressive phase swept up the nation in its wake. The first Red Scare of 1919–1920, stemmed from the nation's first encounter with the Communist Party and its territorial and political designs.[51] With a disabled president sitting in the White House, Wilson's underlings were left to run rampant over the civil liberties of U.S. citizens and alien visitors. Communist Party members were arrested without attention to matching warrants to names or habeas corpus proceedings. Untrustworthy alien visitors were deported quickly; naturalized citizens faced problems in maintaining their citizenship, and American citizens were quickly disabused of their interest in this foreign political party.

This rampage had just begun as the Supreme Court handed down its decision in *Abrams v. United States*,[52] and with that decision, the unanimity of the justices dissolved. Oliver Wendell Holmes, Jr., and Louis D. Brandeis became important dissenters in the cause of free speech, as Holmes wrote, in wartime:

> [W]hen men have realized that time has upset many fighting faiths, they may come to believe even more than they believe the very foundations of their own conduct that the ultimate good desired is better reached by free trade in ideas—that the best test of truth is the power of the thought to get itself accepted in the competition of the market,

[49]249 U.S. 47 (1919).

[50]*Id.* at 50.

[51]*See* PAUL L. MURPHY, THE MEANING OF FREEDOM OF SPEECH: FIRST AMENDMENT FREEDOMS FROM WILSON TO FDR (1972); ROBERT K. MURRAY, RED SCARE: A STUDY OF NATIONAL HYSTERIA, 1919–1920 (1955); WILLIAM PRESTON, JR., ALIENS AND DISSENTERS: FEDERAL SUPPRESSION OF RADICALS, 1903–1933 (2d ed. 1994).

[52]250 U.S. 616 (1919).

> and that truth is the only ground upon which their wishes safely can be carried out.[53]

Here Holmes resurrects the Miltonian concept of the marketplace of ideas and begins presenting the concept that all ideas—even those in opposition to war—should be heard so that the best ideas could survive. Again the reactive cycle reared its head, but it failed to gain acceptance.

The voices of these libertarians were more than matched by those concerned about the safety of the nation. When Attorney General A. Mitchell Palmer asked the Congress to enact a peacetime sedition law, he found supporters. As Senator Thomas Walsh, Democrat of Montana, said, at one time in our history the nation might have:

> allow[ed] the loud-mouthed anarchist freely to express his views and purposes in public, depending upon the general good sense of the people of this country and their attachment to the principles of our Government to counteract whatever possible evil there might be in the assertion; but that time has gone by.[54]

Now, Walsh contended,

> We have in our midst here a vast multitude of people who have no appreciation whatever of our institutions. ... They came here poisoned with political ideas that they have absorbed in the midst of some oppressive, autocratic system of some country in Europe ... and fired with a purpose to ... overthrow all governments.[55]

Congress, he argued, could not let this happen.

But Congress also had its civil libertarians, and their voices became louder. Senator Robert L. Owen, Democrat of Oklahoma, condemned such a measure, saying, "I do not want any bureaucrat in this Government having arbitrary power to lay a rough hand upon a man who is expressing his honest opinion and his belief as to what is the good thing and better the better thing for his fellow citizens."[56] The senator from Oklahoma believed, "It is freedom of opinion, it is freedom of speech, it is freedom of the press, it is freedom of religion

---

[53] *Id.* at 630. *See also* RICHARD POLENBERG, FIGHTING FAITHS: THE ABRAMS CASE, THE SUPREME COURT, AND FREE SPEECH (1987).

[54] 59 CONG. REC. 1322 (1920).

[55] *Id.*

[56] *Id.* at 1774.

and freedom of education which have combined to make this country the greatest free nation in the world."[57] Although the Senate passed a version of a peacetime sedition act, House action was lost as the Red Scare dissipated.

Clearly there were new players on the scene. Eighteenth and nineteenth century issues of suppression had been debated but not with quite the fervor. Concern about the direction the nation was taking reached into the judiciary and into the citizenry. In the days following the end of the Red Scare, the Supreme Court moved more fully into the area of overseeing freedom of expression. By 1925, the justices had added review of state cases that might have involved First Amendment rights to their list of free-expression related activities.[58] By the late 1930s, they had developed a philosophy for dealing with First Amendment issues,[59] and new justices were ready to give new prominence to free-speech topics. Indeed, the Court was more than ready to provide a different approach to dealing with government requests for suppression of free speech during the cycle of concern.

THE TWENTIETH CENTURY EXPERIENCE: THE MIDDLE YEARS

World War II was, of course, the next cycle of concern, but before the nation reached that point, Congress enacted numerous pieces of legislation designed to suppress dissent should the brewing war in Asia and Europe ever involve Americans. Support for the legislation came from both the left and right sides of the aisle. Liberals, generally Democrats, supported the legislative proposals, fearing the possibility of an anti-Semitic movement in the United States. Conservatives, generally Republicans, were not so frightened about any anti-Semitic activities; they were still concerned about the possibility of Communist infiltration. For different reasons, therefore, a substantial majority in both houses established the House Committee on Un-American Activities[60] and enacted legislation ranging

---

[57]*Id.*

[58]*See* Gitlow v. New York, 268 U.S. 652 (1925).

[59]The Court used a footnote in an unrelated case to establish the "preferred position doctrine," which gave the edge in arguments to individuals seeking to prove their rights had been violated as opposed to governments who sought to prove that their laws were necessary. United States v. Carolene Products Co., 304 U.S. 144, 152 n.4 (1938).

[60]*See* WALTER GOODMAN, THE COMMITTEE: THE EXTRAORDINARY CAREER OF THE HOUSE COMMITTEE ON UN-AMERICAN ACTIVITIES (1968); AUGUST RAYMOND OGDEN,

from the Foreign Agents Registration Act of 1938[61] to the Smith Act of 1940.[62]

The Foreign Agents Registration Act required individuals who conducted propaganda activities for a foreign government to reveal their sponsorship to their audience. Considered the peacetime sedition law that was unpassable in the wake of World War I, the Smith Act was designed for use in prosecuting those who were attempting to overthrow the United States government. The fear of native fascism also led Franklin Roosevelt to order an investigation of pro-Nazi groups in the United States in 1934; by 1936, J. Edgar Hoover had won approval to keep tabs on members of the Communist Party as well. Consequently, by 1940, the legislative pieces were in place for the next suppressive cycle.

But a strange thing happened on the way to the next cycle of suppression. The expected suppressive cycle in World War II was badly fractured, if not broken, by unexpected events. To be sure, Franklin Roosevelt, who had been in the Wilson administration during World War I, saw no problem with suppressing certain groups, especially far-right wing dissenters who advocated pro-Nazi views.[63] Eventually, Attorney General Francis Biddle launched a legal attack on American Nazis, but other than that, he successfully blocked efforts to suppress dissent during the war. He made his position very clear even before Pearl Harbor. "We do not lose our right to condemn either measures or men because the country is at war," he told the California Bar shortly after his appointment in summer of 1941.[64] He told the *New York Times* something similar in September:

> In so far as I can, by use of the authority and the influence of my office, I intend to see that civil liberties in this country are protected; that we do not again fall into the disgraceful hysteria of witch hunts, strike break-

---

THE DIES COMMITTEE: A STUDY OF THE SPECIAL HOUSE COMMITTEE FOR THE INVESTIGATION OF UN-AMERICAN ACTIVITIES, 1938–1944 (1945).

[61]H.R. 1591, 75th Cong. (1938).

[62]H.R. 5138, 76th Cong. (1940) (current version U.S.C. 18, ch. 115, § 2386 (2000)).

[63]*See* Leo P. Ribuffo, United States v. McWilliams: *The Roosevelt Administration and the Far Right, in* AMERICAN POLITICAL TRIALS 201–32 (Michal R. Belknap ed., 1981); MAXIMILLAN ST. GEORGE & LAWRENCE DENNIS, A TRIAL ON TRIAL: THE GREAT SEDITION TRIAL OF 1944 (1984); RICHARD W. STEELE, FREE SPEECH IN THE GOOD WAR (1999); PATRICK S. WASHBURN, A QUESTION OF SEDITION: THE FEDERAL GOVERNMENT'S INVESTIGATION OF THE BLACK PRESS DURING WORLD WAR II (1986); Patrick S. Washburn, *FDR Versus His Own Attorney General: The Struggle Over Sedition, 1941–42*, 62 JOURNALISM Q. 717, 717–24 (1985).

[64]Francis Biddle, *The Power of Democracy: It Can Meet All Conditions, in* VITAL SPEECHES, Oct. 15, 1941, at 9.

> ing and minority persecutions which were such a dark chapter in our record of the last World War.[65]

And just to make sure that the message was clearly received, shortly after the attack on Pearl Harbor, he spoke at a Bill of Rights commemoration saying, "[E]very man … who cares about freedom must fight for it for the *other* man with whom he disagrees."[66] Interestingly, Biddle replaced Robert Jackson at the Department of Justice when the latter went to the Supreme Court. Jackson would be the author of perhaps the century's most important freedom of expression decision.

First, however, the Supreme Court hit a patch of bumpy road in 1940, when the justices ruled that local school boards could require Jehovah's Witness children to salute the flag despite their religious beliefs.[67] This was a little more than a year before the United States became involved in World War II, and the nation was jittery. Political and business leaders battled over whether the nation had any business involving itself in a worldwide conflict, and President Wilson's concern about taking a united nation into war was reverberating in Franklin D. Roosevelt's speeches. The children of Walter Gobitis, who were being raised as good Witnesses, soon fell within the crosshairs of this vital argument.

Perhaps, then, it should not have been a surprise when the Court ruled that various political entities within the country could require flag salutes. "National unity is the basis of national security," Justice Felix Frankfurter wrote for an eight-man majority. He added:

> The ultimate foundation of a free society is the binding tie of cohesive sentiment. Such a sentiment is fostered by all those agencies of the mind and spirit which may serve to gather up the traditions of a people, transmit them from generation to generation, and thereby create that continuity of a treasure common life which constitutes a civilization.[68]

Harlan Fiske Stone, who soon would become chief justice, chided those in the majority for violating "the very essence" of liberty as

---

[65]Cabell Phillips, *No Witch Hunts*, N.Y. TIMES MAG., Sept. 21, 1941, at 8.

[66]FRANCIS BIDDLE, IN BRIEF AUTHORITY 211 (1962).

[67]*See* Minersville Sch. Dist. v. Gobitis, 310 U.S. 586 (1940). *See also* Irving J. Dilliard, *The Flag Salute Cases, in* QUARRELS THAT HAVE SHAPED THE CONSTITUTION 222–42 (John A. Garraty ed., 1962); DAVID R. MANWARING, RENDER UNTO CAESAR: THE FLAG SALUTE CONTROVERSY (1962); SHAWN FRANCIS PETERS, JUDGING JEHOVAH'S WITNESSES: RELIGIOUS PERSECUTION AND THE DAWN OF THE RIGHTS REVOLUTION (2000).

[68]*Minersville*, 310 U.S. at 595–96.

guaranteed in the Bill of Rights "in the name of righteousness and the public good." Even worse, Stone wrote, was that most of these infringements were aimed at "politically helpless minorities," when those were the very people the Court was to protect.[69]

Jehovah's Witnesses became the targets of American repressive actions in 1941, and, in 1943, the Court responded with eight Jehovah's Witnesses decisions that reinstated their rights.[70] The reason for the reversal was fairly simple: American treatment of the Witnesses had become a national disgrace, and in a war in which the nation was positioning itself as the "good guy," such behavior could not be allowed to continue. As 1943 approached, Hugo Black, William O. Douglas and Frank Murphy were writing in dissent on Witnesses' cases; they used their prose to publicly apologize for their faulty reasoning in the *Gobitis* case. As the 1943 cases unfolded, the three justices joined in new majorities to protect the rights of these religious itinerants to proseltyze. The reactive cycle was beginning.

By Flag Day 1943, six members of the Court, including several who had been in the majority in *Gobitis*, joined to overturn that decision word-by-word. The decision, which contains what might be the most profound statements ever written about the meaning of patriotism and freedom of expression, remains controversial even today. Jackson, a newcomer to the Court and a Roman Catholic who had substantial intellectual problems with the way in which the Witnesses proselytized, was given the writing assignment. The flag salute, he wrote, clearly "is a form of utterance;" indeed, it was a powerful symbol, a "primitive but effective way of communicating ideas." In fact, "the use of an emblem or flag to symbolize some system, idea, institution, or personality, is a short cut from mind to mind."[71]

National unity surely was important, Jackson admitted, but the state must find other ways to develop love of country. Enforced unity

---

[69]*Id.* at 601, 604.

[70]Jamison v. Texas, 318 U.S. 413 (1943) (declaring an ordinance against distribution of handbills on public streets unconstitutional); Largent v. Texas, 318 U.S. 418 (1943) (declaring a licensing provision unconstitutional); Jones v. Opelika, 319 U.S. 103 (1943) (overturning a year-old decision in the same case and allowing the sale of literature without paying a fee to the municipality); Murdock v. Pennsylvania, 319 U.S. 105 (1943) (allowing sale of religious literature by itinerant preachers without taxation); Martin v. Struthers, 319 U.S. 105 (1943) (allowing Witnesses to knock on doors to proselytize): Douglas v. Jeanette, 319 U.S. 157 (1943) (overturning a requirement that Witnesses be licensed and pay a fee in order to proselytize); Taylor v. Mississippi, 319 U.S. 583 91943) (overturning the conviction of an adult witness for not saluting the flag); West Virginia State Bd. of Educ. v. Barnette, 319 U.S. 624 (1943) (finding a required flag salute unconstitutional).

[71]West Virginia State Bd. of Educ. v. Barnette, 319 U.S. 624, 632 (1943).

of opinion could only lead to disaster. "Those who begin coercive elimination of dissent soon find themselves exterminating dissenters. Compulsory unification of opinions achieves only the unanimity of the graveyard," he wrote.[72] Personally he preferred diversity to uniformity, he wrote, as he added:

> If there is any fixed star in our constitutional constellation, it is that no official, high or petty, can prescribe what shall be orthodox in politics, nationalism, religion, or other matters of opinion or force citizens to confess by word or act their faith therein. If there are any circumstances, which permit an exception, they do not now occur to us.[73]

The question stemming from this brilliant statement of the meaning of patriotism is what did it mean in the history of the Court? Was it a sign that the reactive cycle was in full swing and that World War II decisions would be different from those of World War I? The decision actually marked the beginning of a new way to look at dissent in wartime. The years between World War I and World War II had spawned a greater understanding in freedom of speech than most of its advocates could have imagined; that understanding bore fruit in cases involving dissent in World War II. Two cases are illustrative.

Hartzel v. United States[74] involved an anti-Semite who sent materials directly to members of the armed forces that denounced the British and the Jews and that questioned the president's patriotism. Hartzel was convicted for violating the Espionage Act of 1917, but Justice Frank Murphy wrote for a Court that would not allow the conviction to stand. "We are not unmindful," he wrote:

> [T]hat the United States is now engaged in a total war for national survival and that total war of the modern variety cannot be won by a doubtful, disunited nation in which any appreciable sector is disloyal. For that reason our enemies have developed psychological warfare to a high degree in an effort to cause unrest and disloyalty.[75]

The justices, however, did not find that Hartzel's behavior rose to the level of violation of the Espionage Act. Indeed, Murphy wrote:

---

[72] *Id.*
[73] *Id.* at 641–42.
[74] 322 U.S. 680 (1944).
[75] *Id.* at 689.

> Unless there is sufficient evidence from which a jury could infer beyond a reasonable doubt that he intended to bring about the specific consequences prohibited by the Act, an American citizen has the right to discuss these matters either by temperate reasoning or by immoderate and vicious invective without running afoul of the Espionage Act of 1917.[76]

That was quite a statement for a wartime Court to make. Attempting to encourage disaffection in the armed services merited jail terms in World War I. The change was astounding, especially since Hartzel apparently knew he could be in trouble for distributing his pamphlets. He deposited the envelopes containing the pamphlets in mailboxes around town; he wore protective gloves when he handled the material; he stored extra copies of the pamphlets under his bathtub. That is not the behavior of a man who assumed himself innocent, but the Court did not care about his behavior. In the process of overturning Hartzel's conviction, the justices moved the Court further down the road to a reactive cycle in wartime.

The Court's decision in the Carl Wilhelm Baumgartner case further cemented the right to dissent in wartime. Baumgartner was a naturalized citizen whose loyalty to his new country was questioned after he praised Hitler in a variety of venues. The government sought to revoke Baumgartner's citizenship, but a unanimous Court rejected the effort. "One of the prerogatives of American citizenship is the right to criticize public men and measures—and that means not only informed and responsible criticism, but the freedom to speak foolishly and without moderation," wrote Justice Felix Frankfurter, himself an immigrant.[77] "Our trust in the good sense of the people on deliberate reflection goes deep. For such is the contradictoriness of the human mind that the expression of views which may collide with cherished American ideals does not necessarily prove want of devotion to the Nation."[78]

The reactive cycle had bested the repressive cycle during this war. But how firm was freedom of expression in the wake of World War II? One could argue that it was fairly well established, but one would also have to consider the fact that the *Hartzel* and *Baumgartner* decisions were delivered after the outcome of the war was certain. The

[76]*Id.*

[77]Baumgartner v. United States, 322 U.S. 665, 673–74 (1944).

[78]*Id.* at 674. If the naturalized citizen had taken action against the country, however, that was a different matter. The Court approved revoking the citizenship of Paul Knauer. *See* Knauer v. United States, 328 U.S. 654 (1946).

right to dissent was not established before the war was considered won. Secondly, membership on the Court changed substantially in the postwar years. Even the chief justice was replaced; Stone's replacement was a political colleague of new President Harry S. Truman. Finally, when Robert Jackson returned to the Court after a stint as chief prosecutor at the Nuremberg War Crimes trial, his brilliant prose reflected his newfound fear of the "battle for the streets," which he felt surely was ahead. The Cold War years would surely not continue the reactive cycle of promoting freedom of expression.

For historical purposes, the Cold War began soon after the conclusion of the fighting in World War II. For more practical purposes, it began when members of Congress enacted legislation designed to stop the dissident speech of Communists in the years just prior to the war. Efforts to punish Communists actually had continued through the fighting as anti-Communists sought to have the citizenship of a party official revoked[79] and to deport a labor leader with strong Communist connections.[80] The Supreme Court rebuffed these efforts, finding that the party leader did not necessarily believe everything that the party apparatus wanted him to believe because, after all, "beliefs are personal and not a matter of mere association."[81] In the case of labor leader Harry Bridges, the Court, through the pen of Justice Frank Murphy, reassured non-citizens that aliens had First Amendment rights too. "Many of these aliens," he wrote:

> like many of our forebears, were driven from their original homelands by bigoted authorities who denied the existence of freedom and tolerance. It would be a dismal prospect for them to discover that their freedom in the United States is dependent upon their conformity to the popular notions of the moment.[82]

Indeed, "[t]he Bill of Rights belongs to them as well as to all citizens. ... Only by zealously guarding the rights of the most humble, the most unorthodox and the most despised among us can freedom flourish and endure in our land."[83]

Such sentiments disappeared for the decade after the war as the nation and the Court once again were caught up in a cycle of suppression. The fear of communism grew as the Soviet Union moved into

---

[79] *See* Schneiderman v. United States, 320 U.S. 118 (1943).
[80] *See* Bridges v. Wixon, 326 U.S. 135 (1945).
[81] *Schneiderman,* 320 U.S. at 136.
[82] Bridges v. Wixon, 326 U.S. 135, 166 (1945) (Murphy, J., concurring).
[83] *Id.*

Eastern Europe in the closing days of the war and as anti-Communists fanned the flames of fear through the House Committee on Un-American Activities and later through the McCarthy investigations. President Harry Truman, stunned by accusations that he was soft on Communism, endorsed the creation of a loyalty program that ran rampant throughout the federal bureaucracy. Members of Congress also worked to stifle Communist speakers by enacting the Labor Management Relations Act of 1947,[84] the Internal Security Act of 1950,[85] the Communist Control Act of 1954,[86] and the Immigration and Nationality Act of 1952.[87] Each of these laws was designed to make it much more difficult for members of the Communist Party to function. Basic rights guaranteed to most citizens were denied to Communist Party members, and distribution of party literature became much more difficult.

Starting the reactive phase to the Cold War fear of Communism, strangely enough, was President Truman, who had been responsible for getting at least part of the campaign started. He vetoed both the Internal Security Act and the Immigration and Nationality Act, but his vetoes were overridden by Congress. To a certain extent, the reactive phase needed to be started by someone of the president's stature because of the nationwide concern about Communism. His veto

[84]H.R. 3020, 80th Cong. (1947). Better known as the Taft-Hartley Act, this law was designed to turn back many of the benefits labor unions received through the National Labor Relations Act of 1935. It required all union officials to sign affidavits annually declaring they were not members of the Communist Party. If any official refused to sign, the union involved lost the privilege of using the National Labor Relations Board to help deal with labor disputes.

[85]H.R. 9490, 81st Cong. (1950). This law was aimed at Communist-action and Communist-front organizations. The attorney general was given authority to require groups in either category to register with the Subversive Activities Control Board, which the law established. Registration came after a full hearing and court appeals. It required that the group give the attorney general financial statements and lists of officers. If the group had been labeled a Communist-action organization, a list of members also would be required. Members of registered organizations could be barred from employment in certain industries as well as be banned from foreign travel.

[86]S. 3706, 83d Cong. (1954). This law formally outlawed the Communist Party. Under its terms each member could be subjected to fines and jail sentences upon conviction of such membership. The law created substantial problems for federal prosecutors because of Fifth Amendment protections against self-incrimination. If a party organization registered, as required under the Internal Security Act of 1950, it was clearly indicating that its officers and members had violated the Communist Control Act.

[87]H.R. 5678, 82nd Cong. (1952). Better known as the McCarran-Walter Act, the measure completely rewrote the nation's immigration law. One of its goals was to make it easier to deport current, former and alleged Communists. It also tightened provisions for entering the country and made it more difficult to become a citizen.

messages clearly showed his remorse over his earlier actions, although by 1950 Truman was just one player in the nation's macabre dance with Communism. "In a free country," he proclaimed, "we punish men for the crimes they commit, but never for the opinions they have." The reason for this protection, he said, is not to safeguard minorities but "[t]o permit freedom of expression … for the benefit of the majority, because it protect criticism, and criticism leads to progress."[88] Truman's conversion came too late. By his 1952 veto of the Immigration and Nationality Act, he was on his way out of office. The Republicans who controlled the Congress were about to control the White House as well.

Some Republicans in the United States Senate, unhappy with McCarthy's behavior, tried to rein him in early in his career. Margaret Chase Smith, Republican of Maine, denounced senators who sought to deny freedom of speech to others. She said:

> Those of us who shout the loudest about Americanism in making character assassinations are all too frequently those who, by our own words and acts, ignore some of the basic principles of Americanism—The right to criticize. The right to hold unpopular beliefs. The right to protest. The right of independent thought.[89]

She and seven other Republican senators combined to put forth a "Declaration of Conscience," condemning the anti-Communist witch-hunts being pursued by members of the Senate. Senator Smith's campaign was lost in the start of the Korean War on June 25, 1950, and Senator McCarthy continued his witch-hunts until his censure by the Senate in December 1954. The action was for his disregard of the dignity of the Senate.

The Supreme Court, safely in the hands of Chief Justice Earl Warren, launched an attack on congressional investigations and, on June 17, 1957, handed down four decisions in which the rights of Communists were vindicated.[90] There were no ringing or memorable words in these decisions—just statements parsing laws more carefully and criticizing Congress for its investigatory techniques. That decision day was quickly labeled "Red Monday" by pundits

---

[88]Harry S. Truman, *Veto of the Internal Security Bill,* PUB. PAPERS 649–59 (Sept. 22, 1950).

[89]104 CONG. REC. 7894 (1950).

[90]Watkins v. United States, 354 U.S. 178 (1957); Sweezy v. New Hampshire, 354 U.S. 234 (1957); Yates v. United States, 354 U.S. 298 (1957); Service v. Dulles, 354 U.S. 363 (1957). For a discussion of these cases, *see* ARTHUR J. SABIN, IN CALMER TIMES: THE SUPREME COURT AND RED MONDAY (1999).

and congressional critics alike as debate built over restricting the Court's jurisdiction. The Warren Court had made more enemies than friends with its decisions on school desegregation and its explorations of the rights of criminals. Decisions appearing to benefit Communists seemed like one too many new fronts for the Supreme Court. The justices quietly retreated from protecting Communists and pursued other areas of interest. Nevertheless, by 1974, a unanimous Court declared for various reasons that Indiana had acted unconstitutionally when it denied the Communist Party a place on the ballot.[91]

Support for Communist hunters at all levels of government, in private industry and in the general public was the dominant position during these years. Opposition to such witch-hunts came sporadically from individuals with impeccable reputations but did not last long. The Cold War years may well have been the most effective cycle of suppression in United States history, and the reactive cycle may well have been the weakest and least effective. We could say that ten to fifteen years of suppression during the Cold War likely is not excessive, given the world situation at the time. Or we could look more fully for progress in freedom of expression in other areas to find hope for that reactive cycle of the future, and it is in the civil rights movement and the antiwar movement of the 1960s and 1970s that we can find the kernels of that reactive cycle.

THE TWENTIETH CENTURY EXPERIENCE: THE LATER YEARS

The nugget of free speech that the Supreme Court sought to preserve in the wake of Red Monday dealt with freedom of expression for individuals pursuing civil rights in the South. Southern defeats in *Brown I*[92] and *Brown II*[93] led the legislators and governors to seek ways to punish the NAACP for its behavior. New laws were passed, and old legislation was dusted off. Each was designed to tie the NAACP up in court while it fought repressive legislation, for the NAACP would stop its activities in a state until it had won the legal right to start business there once more. Toward the end of the 1950s, the NAACP won First Amendment protection for its membership list, with the Court holding that names of members in the South could be kept confidential to protect them from harassment.[94] It had

[91]*See* Communist Party of Indiana v. Whitcomb, 414 U.S. 441 (1974).
[92]Brown v. Board of Education 347 U.S. 483 (1954).
[93]Brown v. Board of Education 349 U.S. 294 (1955).
[94]*See* NAACP v. Alabama, 357 U.S. 449 (1958).

used the First Amendment to fend off requirements that every teacher in a state-supported school or college annually file an affidavit listing every organization the employee had belonged to during the previous five years.[95] And it convinced the Court that there was a First Amendment right to band together to seek legal redress in the courts.[96] The Court's goal in these and other cases of the period was to keep the southern states from suppressing the voice of the civil rights movement. The justices were deeply convinced of the need to promote civil rights, and ensuring the ability of individuals to be heard about their grievances in the South served that purpose. Such concern also worked to protect members of the press because the justices wanted journalists free to tell the segregation story in all of its gory details. Protection from libel came as a result of that concern.[97] As the NAACP withdrew from the South to fight in the courtrooms, a more active civil rights movement took its place.

If we were to continue our tour through repressive and reactive cycles as we have in previous periods, we would find the president and Congress again being repressive. President John F. Kennedy tried to stop journalists from reporting what they personally witnessed about the Vietnam War.[98] Lyndon B. Johnson told such lies about the Vietnam War that journalists referred to the "credibility gap" between what the president said about the war and what reporters on the ground could see for themselves.[99] And Richard M. Nixon called upon his "silent majority" to back him in a variety of actions to suppress dissenters.[100]

Congress, badly divided over Civil Rights and antiwar issues, kept pace with the presidents of the era in reacting to discord of the times. Its legislation was not as suppressive as it had been in World War I, just before World War II or during the Cold War, but its purpose was clear. Offended by antiwar protesters who burned their draft cards as a challenge to establishment war plans, members of Congress amended legislation to make it criminal to destroy a draft card.[101] Mendel Rivers, the powerful head of the House Armed Services Com-

[95]*See* Shelton v. Tucker, 364 U.S. 479 (1960).

[96]*See* NAACP v. Button, 371 U.S. 415 (1963).

[97]*See* New York Times v. Sullivan, 376 U.S. 254 (1964) (creating the actual malice defense for libel).

[98]*See* MARGARET A. BLANCHARD, REVOLUTIONARY SPARKS: FREEDOM OF INFORMATION IN MODERN AMERICA 281 (1992).

[99]*Id.* at 321.

[100]*Id.* at 333.

[101]H.R. 10306, 76th Cong. (1940) (as amended 79 Stat. 58679 Stat. 586 (1965) (2001)).

mittee, believed the law was essential. "It is a straightforward clear answer to those who would make a mockery of our efforts in South Vietnam by engaging in the mass destruction of draft cards," he said. Further, Rivers asserted:

> [I]f it can be proved that a person knowingly destroyed or mutilated his draft card, then ... he can be sent to prison, where he belongs. This is the least we can do for our men in South Vietnam fighting to preserve freedom, while a vocal minority in this country thumb their noses at their own Government.[102]

Unhappy that a roving core of antiwar radicals traveled the country speaking to crowds of young people and sparking antiwar protests, Congress enacted the Safe Streets Act of 1968,[103] which made it a crime to cross state lines to foment a riot. And, displeased by the number of demonstrations that occurred on the Capitol grounds, members of Congress pulled out a 1946 law that prohibited certain activities there and stiffened provisions so that antiwar protests were prohibited.[104]

Presidents were not terribly successful in suppressing the rising wave of dissent that gripped the land. Only Nixon showed the anti-press stamina necessary to almost win that battle, only to stumble over the debris left by the Watergate break-in. Congressional efforts likewise failed more than they succeeded. The Supreme Court upheld the anti-draft card burning measure,[105] but in other areas, justices widened the ability of individuals to protest either for civil rights or against the war. Supreme Court reaction to suppressive actions by other branches of government ranged from widening the concept of conscientious objector status[106] and halting retaliatory classification efforts by the Selective Service in their tracks.[107] In ad-

---

[102]111 CONG. REC. 19871 (1965).

[103]Omnibus Crime Control and Safe Street Act of 1968, Pub. L. No. 90–351, 82 Stat. 197 (1968) (current version 42 U.S.C. § 3789d (2002)).

[104]S. 2310, 90th Cong. (1967).

[105]*See* United States v. O'Brien, 391 U.S. 367 (1966).

[106]*See* Gillette v. United States, 401 U.S. 437 (1971) (conscientious objectors must be opposed to all wars, not just the one in Vietnam); Welsh v. United States, 398 U.S. 33 (1970) (conscientious objector status may be based in public policy beliefs); United States v. Seeger, 380 U.S. 163 (1965) (belief in a supreme being that holds a parallel place in a person's life to the more orthodox belief in God).

[107]*See* Breen v. Selective Service Bd., 396 U.S. 460 (1970) (a person with a student classification returned his draft card and was reclassified as a result); Gutknecht v. United States, 396 U.S. 295 (1970) (a student was appealing his IA classification when he returned his draft card); Oesterich v. Selective Service Sys., 393 U.S. 233 (1968) (a theological student returned his draft card and was reclassified as a result).

dition, the justices allowed foul language to appear on the back of leather jackets[108] and supported various kinds of protests, including those of children.[109] The Court also started on a line of cases that led the justices to the flag-burning cases of the 1980s and 1990s.[110]

The language may not have been as stirring as it had been earlier, for few members of the Court had the literary skills of Holmes, Brandeis, Black, Douglas and Jackson, but members of the Court kept busy during the 1960s and early 1970s on topics that clearly showed their interest in preserving an open society that includes free debate. Interestingly, some of the best commentary preserving free speech came from lower courts:

- An appeals court hearing the case involving congressional action to preserve the park-like quality of the Capitol grounds held: "The desire of Congress, if such be, to function in the 'serenity' of a 'park-like setting' is fundamentally at odds with the principles of the First Amendment."[111]
- An appeals court hearing the case of the Boston Five, which included Dr. Benjamin Spock and Yale University Chaplain William Sloane Coffin as defendants, said in overturning the convictions: "Inseparable from the question of the sufficiency of the evidence to convict are the rights of the defendants, and others, under the First Amendment."[112]
- An appeals court hearing arguments on the convictions of the Chicago Seven for violating the Safe Streets Act, among other things, addressed the issue of rioting:

> [R]ioting, in history and by nature, almost invariably occurs as an expression of political, social, or economic reactions, if not ideas. The rioting assemblage is usually protesting the policies of a govern-

[108]*See* Cohen v. California, 403 U.S. 15 (1971) (wearing a profanity on a black leather jacket in a California public courthouse).

[109]*See* Tinker v. Des Moines Indep. Cmty. Sch. Dist., 393 U.S. 503 (1969) (permitting students in public schools to wear black armbands in protest of the Vietnam War).

[110]*See* Smith v. Goguen, 415 U.S. 566 (1974) (wearing a replica of the American flag sewn on the seat of blue jeans); Spence v. Washington, 418 U.S. 405 (1974) (peace symbol placed on a personal flag, flag hung upside down on private property as a protest of the killings at Kent State); Street v. New York, 394 U.S. 576 (1969) (African-American man burning personal flag as a protest for the shooting of James Meredith).

[111]Jeanette Rankin Brigade v. Chief of Capitol Police, 342 F. Supp. 575, 585 (D.C.D.C. 1972).

[112]United States v. Spock, 416 F.2d 165, 169 (1st Cir. 1969).

> ment, an employer, or some other institution, or the social fabric in general, as was probably the case in the riots of 1967 and 1968, which are the backdrop for this legislation.[113]

In addition, the court noted:

> [A] riot may well erupt out of an originally peaceful demonstration which many participants intended to maintain as such. Each participant is entitled to a careful distinction between responsibility for the lawful and constitutionally protected demonstration and responsibility for the activity for which the legislative body validly prescribe a penalty.[114]

Although the Safe Streets Act was upheld as constitutional, most of the convictions were overturned, and there were no retrials.

One interesting aspect of these cases is that they were not United States Supreme Court cases. However, the decisions measured the importance of protecting freedom of speech. The message about the importance of dissenting had clearly made its way throughout the judicial system and, by the end of the war, had made incursion into the ranks of Congress as well. The executive branch, intent on protecting its policies remained substantially opposed to freedom of speech and maintained the suppressive line of discussion mentioned throughout this essay.

Perhaps of even greater importance is the fact that during these years, the individual American became the key to a new wave of civil disobedience that occupied stools at lunch counters and burned draft records. Catholic priests and pediatricians. College students and public school students. Black and white. Male and female. The reactive cycle belonged more to them than to anyone else, for they were the ones who were demanding the right to behave in ways unacceptable to many in power. It is true that individual Americans had protested before, but most of those earlier protesters had some sort of formal tie to the issue being protested. Here, the decision was being made individually based on individual assessments of the situation. Suppression clearly would never be the same again.

CONCLUSION

Siebert was clearly correct when he postulated that the amount of repression of expression increases coincidentally with the degree of

[113]United States v. Dellinger, 472 F.2d 340, 359 (7th Cir. 1972).
[114]*Id.*

instability of government and society. What he did not see, perhaps because it was not apparent in the time period he was studying, was that an increased amount of repression—at least in American society—gives rise to an effort to redress the balance in favor of freedom of speech. Essentially, this means that repression of speech can last only so long before there is a demand from some part of society for greater freedom of speech. Further, this occurrence seems to take the form of cycles rather than lineal development. The cycle of repression develops first, and then the cycle of reaction follows soon thereafter. Eventually, the reactive cycle becomes the dominant one. It falls victim to the next period of governmental and societal instability. Then the process starts all over again.

With this said, however, many questions remain about this cyclical aspect of freedom of speech. Of particular concern, one would suppose, is whether there is a predictive value to these cycles. Can, for instance, we see warning signs on the horizon that will allow us to fend off the next suppressive cycle? Or, is there anything that can be done to hurry the development of the reactive cycles? These questions are beyond the scope of this paper, and perhaps they are not answerable.

Perhaps one question that needs to be addressed more quickly stems from my student's query: Why can we not learn from previous repressive and reactive cycles? Why are the lessons not firmly burned into our brains so that we at least do not repeat past mistakes? In an era dominated by the USA Patriot Act, Americans should concentrate on how to start the inevitable reactive cycle. A discussion along these lines may well be the most profitable one of all.

7 COMM. L. & POL'Y 379–399 (2002)

FREDRICK SIEBERT'S ABSOLUTE, ADJUSTABLE FIRST AMENDMENT

JEFFERY A. SMITH*

Fredrick Siebert is known for his analysis of the role of "stresses" in shaping freedom of expression. How flexible did he think First Amendment rights should be? His career and writings are examined to identify his positions and to understand how they may have been formed. Siebert believed that the founders were absolutists on government restraints, and he questioned subsequent efforts to define liberties in other ways. Like a scholar who influenced his career, Willard Bleyer, Siebert was a prominent journalism educator who could be a critic of the media. While Bleyer complained about communication monopolies and called for self-regulation, Siebert generally took a libertarian approach. He wanted protection for the business interests of the press and few, if any, government restrictions on content.

Knowing the long record of human failures, the framers of the Constitution did not envision a utopia, but rather an ungainly governmental system that would attempt to subdue selfish and self-defeating impulses. The goals of the Preamble often would have to be sought at the expense of individual freedom. Making a democracy work, however, required recognizing a special class of rights, the rights of expression exercised by citizens and their public servants. Checks and balances might make sense for the three official branches, but the independent fourth branch, the press, had to be free from interference by the other three in order to operate effectively. Early Americans often extolled freedom of expression, but the founders were divided over the question of whether the Constitution should have an explicit press protection. Opponents of a bill of rights

*Professor, Department of Journalism and Mass Communication, University of Wisconsin–Milwaukee.

said the proposed federal government had limited, listed powers that did not reach the right to publish. James Madison, a reluctant convert to written guarantees, and others worried that constitutional barriers could not stop the violation of essential liberties during wars and other crises.[1]

Madison's fears, of course, were justified even though the states ratified a Constitution saying that Congress makes all laws and a First Amendment saying Congress shall make no law abridging freedom of the press. Regarding safety as a higher law than the Constitution, Congress passed laws abridging freedom of expression, and the president and military restricted the flow of information to the public. The Supreme Court did little to interfere. Scholars sometimes questioned the use of prerogative power for suppression, but many were drifting away from the democratic faith in reason and republican virtue.[2] Rights, they often thought, had to be understood in the context of shifting social forces and balanced with identified needs. During the twentieth century, legal formalism and classic libertarian values were extensively critiqued. Interdisciplinary approaches to law and corresponding theories of First Amendment jurisprudence proliferated.[3]

One of the scholars who grappled with the increasingly incoherent concept of press freedom was Fredrick Seaton Siebert, a legal historian who studied five centuries of the development of freedom of expression beginning in England. Siebert's publications, which appeared from the 1920s to the 1970s, analyzed the forms and dynamics of suppression in ways that highlighted fundamental conflicts and contradictions. Writing about such sensitive issues at a time of extraordinary national changes and anxieties was difficult, especially for someone like Siebert, who valued liberty, lucidity of thought and his own reputation. His views on First Amendment interpretation have been neglected, perhaps because they were presented in brief statements scattered among his works. He intended to write two books about the evolution of press freedom in the United

[1]*See generally* JEFFERY A. SMITH, PRINTERS AND PRESS FREEDOM: THE IDEOLOGY OF EARLY AMERICAN JOURNALISM (1988).

[2]*See generally* JEFFERY A. SMITH, WAR AND PRESS FREEDOM: THE PROBLEM OF PREROGATIVE POWER (1999).

[3]*See generally* MATTHEW D. BUNKER, CRITIQUING FREE SPEECH: FIRST AMENDMENT THEORY AND THE CHALLENGE OF INTERDISCIPLINARITY (2001). After noting that the "no law" language of the First Amendment has been considered inconsistent with needs and practices, one scholar has observed that judges and scholars have been "left largely adrift on a sea of possible interpretations" and "have often been inclined to clutch at anything within reach with the least appearance of logical buoyancy." LEE C. BOLLINGER, THE TOLERANT SOCIETY 5–6 (1986).

States, but did not complete them. Was he simply a "balancer" who gave "no encouragement" to absolutists, as one scholar has claimed?[4] How far did Siebert's criticism of public or private constraints go, and how were his conclusions formed? How were his biography and bibliography intertwined?

BIOGRAPHY

Human consciousness allows individuals to learn, review and create a variety of guiding images for solving problems and taking actions.[5] A characteristic of gifted thinkers is their ability to remain open to experience and to tolerate contradictions as they work on solutions.[6] Fredrick Siebert displayed an uncommonly accommodating intellectual temperament as he applied historical evidence, legal logic and professional standards to issues involving freedom of the press. Often critical of media controls and sometimes of press performance, he could appreciate the advantages of both First Amendment absolutism and balancing as well as robust dispute and social responsibility. Siebert could respect aspects of an assortment of approaches, but generally favored the path of least restraint for expression. He did not think anyone could claim a monopoly on truth and backed remarkably broad interpretations of the press clause.

In "A Belated Diary," written for his children and grandchildren when he was in his seventies, Siebert reminisced about what he described as a happy childhood.[7] Born in a log house in 1901 or 1902 (the unregistered birth left him uncertain about the year),[8] he lived in several small, ethnically diverse communities in northern Minnesota and for two years in a village in western Canada.[9] The adults he knew valued their freedom from Old World limitations and gave him

[4]Charles Marler, *Fredrick S. Siebert and the Legal Method*, *in* MAKERS OF THE MEDIA MIND: JOURNALISM EDUCATORS AND THEIR IDEAS 189 (Wm. David Sloan ed., 1990). For examples of Siebert not being included in general discussions of First Amendment historians, see Gaspare J. Saladino, *The Bill of Rights: A Bibliographic Essay*, *in* CONTEXTS OF THE BILL OF RIGHTS 84–89 (Stephen L. Schechter & Richard B. Bernstein eds., 1990); Wm. David Sloan & Thomas A. Schwartz, *Freedom of the Press, 1690–1801: Libertarian or Limited?* 5 AM. JOURNALISM 159 (1988).

[5]*See* ANTONIO DAMASIO, THE FEELING OF WHAT HAPPENS: BODY AND EMOTION IN THE MAKING OF CONSCIOUSNESS 23–25 (1999).

[6]*See* Patricia Haensly et al., *Giftedness: Coalescence, Context, Conflict, and Commitment*, *in* CONCEPTIONS OF GIFTEDNESS 128–48 (Robert J. Sternberg & Janet E. Davidson eds., 1986).

[7]Fredrick Seaton Siebert, A Belated Diary 23 (1976, 1979) (unpublished manuscript, Siebert Papers, State Historical Society of Wisconsin).

[8]*Id.* at 1–2.

[9]*Id.* at 2, 5, 37, 43, 51–53, 65.

an education in freedom of thought and expression. His father, Frank, a sausage maker, was born in Germany where he developed a strong dislike of militarism during compulsory military service.[10] Fred's mother, Sarah, also had a subversive streak that was displayed when the family was in Canada. Irritated by the social pretensions of the British-bred citizens who celebrated the king's birthday, she dressed Fred in an Uncle Sam suit on the Fourth of July and had him gallop a horse up and down the street while shooting his cap gun.[11] Political demonstrations were not unheard of in the small town. The boy remembered seeing Dukhobors, a religious sect that fled persecution in Russia, protest any infringement of their rights by parading naked in public.[12]

Siebert had warm, vivid memories of the varied influences in his youth in the rowdy Minnesota mining range. He knew an assortment of colorful characters[13] and delivered meat to a brothel where the women gave him candy.[14] His parents admired Robert M. "Fighting Bob" La Follette,[15] the progressive political reformer who opposed American involvement in World War I. Frank Siebert, who blamed German militarism for the conflict, kept track of the army movements with pins placed on a large map of Europe.[16] Fred was drafted, but was relieved that the war ended before he reached the required age.[17] Although his parents struggled financially,[18] he had a good education in schools supported by the mineral wealth of the region.[19] Sarah's father, whose parents were English Quakers,[20] and her husband[21] brought a love of reading to family life. Profanity and off-color jokes were forms of entertainment among the relatives,[22] but Fred was steered carefully by his mother whose parents and sisters had helped her hide the birth of a child before marriage.[23] Sarah and Fred had a close and loving relationship. She took him to Sunday mass and repeatedly warned him about the perils of venereal disease, a common

[10] *Id.* at 6.
[11] *Id.* at 46–47.
[12] *Id.* at 46.
[13] *Id.* at 29.
[14] *Id.* at 24.
[15] *Id.* at 67.
[16] *Id.* at 55.
[17] *Id.* at 64.
[18] *Id.* at 52.
[19] *Id.* at 58.
[20] *Id.* at 9.
[21] *Id.* at 12, 69–70.
[22] *Id.* at 27, 69.
[23] *Id.* at 61.

affliction in the mining towns.[24] She wanted her son to be an attorney, and the young man dutifully made plans for law school.[25]

During his college years, Siebert learned about both lofty principles of behavior and some of the more disreputable realities. He obtained a scholarship from the University of Wisconsin and enrolled in its journalism school in the fall of 1920.[26] He took classes from Willard "Daddy" Bleyer,[27] an influential educator who stressed the importance of informative reporting in a democracy and who advocated social science and humanities approaches for journalism professors and students. Bleyer promoted socially responsible press behavior and hoped to bring more respectability to the study of journalism. As he built a program at Wisconsin modeled on his beliefs[28] he emphasized the need "to protect society and government against immature, half-educated, unscrupulous journalists"[29] and to condemn "news and editorial policies designed merely to advance the personal, political, or class interests of publishers."[30] Bleyer criticized monopolistic media and called for organizations that would establish high professional standards.[31] He could be outspoken, but was widely admired as a gentleman and scholar. After Bleyer's death in 1935, a Wisconsin student and colleague, Ralph O. Nafziger, said he was remembered as "fundamentally honest, sincere, good-natured, fearless and never vindictive."[32]

Siebert had a similar willingness to be both congenial and critical, but he placed more emphasis on civil liberties than social responsibilities. His diary displays a nonjudgmental interest in human foibles and in the difficulties of maintaining moral codes. He wrote about spending the summer and fall of 1921 in Minnesota working for "Dad" Atkinson, the owner of the *Hibbing Daily News*. Atkinson upset city officials with acerbic editorials and had two family households, one with his wife and another with a mistress.[33] Siebert

---

[24]*Id.* at 42, 68.

[25]*Id.* at 58, 70.

[26]*Id.* at 67, 70.

[27]*Id.* at 77.

[28]*See* Donald K. Ross, *Willard G. Bleyer and Journalism Education*, 34 JOURNALISM Q. 466 (1957).

[29]Willard Grosvenor Bleyer, *What Journalism Schools are Trying to Do*, 8 JOURNALISM Q. 35, 37 (1931).

[30]Willard Grosvenor Bleyer, *Freedom of the Press and the New Deal*, 11 JOURNALISM Q. 22, 33 (1934).

[31]*See* Willard G. Bleyer, *The Greatest Weakness*, 4 JOURNALISM Q. 15 (1928).

[32]Ralph O. Nafziger, *Willard G. Bleyer, 1875–1935*, 12 JOURNALISM Q. 374, 377 (1935).

[33]*See* Siebert, *supra* note 7, at 79–80.

enjoyed covering the local professional baseball team that hired players suspended from the 1919 Chicago "Black Sox" team.[34]

Back on the Madison campus, where he worked at the *Daily Cardinal*, Siebert admired the renowned professors who taught undergraduate classes and was intrigued by the sexual freedom and speak-easies of a Roaring Twenties university.[35] He attributed the shift in moral standards mainly to Prohibition, a legal restriction with unintended consequences.[36] He graduated in 1923 and took a faculty position at Bradley Polytechnic Institute in Peoria.[37] The city was strongly Roman Catholic, he noted, but leading citizens were keeping mistresses. He advised the Newman Club and sent money to his parents, but also patronized the brothels and illegal drinking establishments.[38]

As his scholarship and the work of sociologists of the law would later show, Siebert recognized that rules often did not control human behavior. He could empathize with those who had minds of their own, such as his father, the Dukhobors, "Fighting Bob" La Follette, "Dad" Atkinson and "Daddy" Bleyer. Yet, like his mother, he wanted the esteem of others. Colleagues appreciated him for being supportive and intellectually stimulating. Still, Siebert was free-spirited enough to hitchhike to conferences long after he could afford the transportation.[39] Leslie G. Moeller, the long-time director of the journalism school at the University of Iowa, said that Siebert was "very skillful in personal relationships, excellent in explaining, and very good in persuasion."[40] Siebert regarded Willard Bleyer as the most important influence on his career.[41] He spoke of Bleyer's devotion to research, his authorship of a "comprehensive" history of American journalism[42] and his efforts to "sell" university training for journalists.[43]

Bleyer began promoting journalism education in the 1890s, when he was an undergraduate at the University of Wisconsin and editor

---

[34]*Id.* at 80.

[35]*Id.* at 72, 74, 77, 82.

[36]*Id.* at 82.

[37]*Id.* at 82, 9–1.

[38]*Id.* at 9–6, 9–7.

[39]*See* Everett M. Rogers & Steven H. Chaffee, *Communication and Journalism from "Daddy" Bleyer to Wilbur Schramm: A Palimpsest*, 148 JOURNALISM MONOGRAPHS 1, 17, 21 (1994).

[40]W. J. Zima & Gary Wade, Interview with Leslie G. Moeller 20 (1970) (unpublished transcript, AEJMC Papers, State Historical Society of Wisconsin).

[41]Robert V. Hudson, Interview with Fredrick Seaton Siebert 2, 3 (1970) (unpublished transcript, AEJMC Papers, State Historical Society of Wisconsin).

[42]*Id.* at 3.

[43]*Id.* at 9.

of the *Daily Cardinal*. He earned a Ph.D. at Wisconsin, joined its English faculty, and eventually developed a separate journalism program. He also did public relations work for the campus and cultivated relationships with the newspaper industry.[44] Although known as a dull lecturer, Bleyer was a dynamic leader in journalism education organizations.[45] He wrote textbooks and traveled extensively to find sources for his 1927 textbook *Main Currents in the History of American Journalism*.[46] Believing in "the importance of English journalism as an influence on American journalism previous to 1800,"[47] he spent the summer of 1923 studying newspapers at the British Museum.[48] The textbook focuses on great men and their newspapers in a rather Whiggish story of progress toward the present but ends elegiacally. The publishing business, Bleyer lamented, had become generally aimed at "giving the public what it wanted to read"[49] and delivered a product that "showed the effect of the superficiality and standardization everywhere manifested in American life."[50] He saw hope in the creation of journalism schools, the formation of ethics codes and attempts to organize labor unions and professional societies for journalists.[51]

Like other pioneering journalism educators,[52] Siebert regarded Bleyer as a visionary, but did not always take the same directions. Siebert was less concerned about media monopolies and commercialism and more knowledgeable about communication law. (Bleyer was naive enough to write in 1934 that America's press had been "completely free for over a century and a quarter" with the exception of some "trifling" wartime restrictions.[53]) Siebert's interests were more likely to be societal controls than the industry self-regulation Bleyer wanted. Siebert's legal scholarship flourished after he left Bradley in 1926 for the University of Illinois School of Journalism where he taught communication law.[54] Following his mother's wishes, he

[44]Ross, *supra* note 28, at 466–69.

[45]James L. Baughman, *Willard Grosvenor Bleyer*, 3 AM. NAT'L BIOGRAPHY 18–19 (John A. Garraty & Mark C. Carnes eds., 1999).

[46]Nafziger, *supra* note 32, at 375.

[47]WILLARD GROSVENOR BLEYER, MAIN CURRENTS IN THE HISTORY OF AMERICAN JOURNALISM iii (1927).

[48]*Id.* at iv.

[49]*Id.* at 429.

[50]*Id.*

[51]*Id.* at 426–29.

[52]*See* Rogers & Chaffee, *supra* note 39; WILBUR SCHRAMM, THE BEGINNINGS OF COMMUNICATION STUDY IN AMERICA: A PERSONAL MEMOIR 137 (Steven H. Chaffee & Everett M. Rogers eds., 1997).

[53]Bleyer, *supra* note 30, at 34.

[54]*The Directory of Teachers*, JOURNALISM BULL., Jan. 1927, at 37.

earned a J.D. from the university's law school in 1929 and was admitted to the state bar.[55] Following Bleyer's beckoning to research, he began publishing work that was often impressively documented, but lacking in Bleyeresque passion. Siebert was more analytical and more inclined to see more than one side of an issue.

Siebert's 1928 *Journalism Quarterly* article on "Contempt of Court and the Press" impressed Col. Robert McCormick, a lawyer and the publisher of the *Chicago Tribune*. McCormick, who exemplified many of the journalistic sins Bleyer preached against, was spearheading the defense of Jay Near, a scandal sheet publisher who was appealing a prior restraint decision to the Supreme Court of the United States. A Minnesota public nuisance law had been used to prohibit Near from continuing the publication of a weekly that dramatized stories of crime and corruption, often with slurs and complaints that the press and politicians were not protecting the public. Not unfamiliar with hard-hitting crusading himself, McCormick invited Siebert to lunch in his private dining room at the *Tribune*'s Gothic office building to talk about the case. At McCormick's office he could read the *Chicago Tribune*'s credo on the large marble fireplace: "The Newspaper is an Institution developed by Modern Civilization to present the News of the day, to foster Commerce and Industry, to inform and lead Public Opinion, and to furnish that check upon Government which no Constitution has ever been able to provide." Siebert agreed to write a research paper on the history of press freedom to be incorporated into the brief and he attended conferences at the publisher's law firm.[56]

The prior restraint statute was found unconstitutional in *Near v. Minnesota*,[57] and Siebert felt "flattered to have a small part in this landmark case,"[58] but he could not muster much enthusiasm for the seamy side of Minnesota journalism. He said a "gang" published Near's *Saturday Press*, and he traced the origin of the state law to an acquaintance who had been blackmailed by John Morrison, the nearly destitute editor of the Duluth *Rip-Saw*.[59] Morrison attacked the rampant vice and graft in Minnesota, but made money by agreeing, for a

[55]Fred S. Siebert, *My Experiences with the First Amendment*, 56 JOURNALISM Q. 446, 446 (1979).

[56]FRED W. FRIENDLY, MINNESOTA RAG: THE DRAMATIC STORY OF THE LANDMARK SUPREME COURT CASE THAT GAVE NEW MEANING TO FREEDOM OF THE PRESS 75–77 (Vintage Books 1982) (1981).

[57]283 U.S. 697 (1931).

[58]Siebert, *supra* note 55, at 447.

[59]*Id*. at 446.

price, to pull some of his punches.[60] Siebert presumably learned about Morrison during his Bradley years when he had a summer job at the Duluth *Herald*.[61] Siebert did not express much admiration for McCormick either. "Col. McCormick had for many years been a 'freedom of the press' buff and had written several articles and pamphlets on the subject," Siebert dryly noted.[62] McCormick was chairman of the Committee on Freedom of the Press of the American Newspaper Publishers Association and had shamed and cajoled almost all of the members to endorse Near's appeal. Several of the holdouts seem to have been from Minnesota where journalists had been among those supporting passage of the "gag law."[63] (Justice Pierce Butler, a Minnesota native, wrote the dissenting opinion in the *Near* case.[64]) McCormick celebrated his court victory in a nationwide radio address from Thomas Jefferson's Monticello. He made a fervent speech, arguing that principles of liberty must not be sacrificed to expediency.[65]

Siebert also supported freedom of expression, but, as a Bleyer student, he cared enough about journalistic scruples not to applaud defaming, disreputable journalists in his home state or a smug Chicago publisher who could misuse the freedom he promoted. The relationship with McCormick proved beneficial, however. Siebert wanted to spend a sabbatical year in England doing research on the British origins of the First Amendment and asked him for help. McCormick, who for years had been studying the history of freedom of expression himself, arranged for an ANPA grant and wrote letters of introduction, one of which helped Siebert obtain important Stationers Company records.[66] (Siebert's 1952 book based on the research acknowledged ANPA funding, but did not mention McCormick's role in obtaining it or in gaining access to previously unused sources.[67]) Siebert also followed Bleyer's footsteps to the

---

[60]Reed L. Carpenter, *John L. Morrison and the Origins of the Minnesota Gag Law*, 9 JOURNALISM HIST. 16, 16–17, 25–28 (1982).

[61]Siebert, *supra* note 7, at 9–7.

[62]Siebert, *supra* note 55, at 447.

[63]*See* FRIENDLY, *supra* note 56, at 88–90; Carpenter, *supra* note 60, at 26. A number of the state's editors and publishers held public office or public service positions at the time. Patricia L. Dooley, *Minnesota Publishers and Editors as Elected Officials, 1923–1938: A Comparison of Journalistic Rhetoric and Conduct*, 71 JOURNALISM Q. 64 (1994).

[64]Near v. Minnesota, 283 U.S. 697, 723 (1931) (Butler, J., dissenting).

[65]RICHARD NORTON SMITH, THE COLONEL: THE LIFE AND LEGEND OF ROBERT R. MCCORMICK, 1880–1955, 284–85 (1997).

[66]Siebert, *supra* note 55, at 447.

[67]FREDRICK SEATON SIEBERT, FREEDOM OF THE PRESS IN ENGLAND 1476–1776: THE RISE AND DECLINE OF GOVERNMENT CONTROL viii (1952).

British Museum.[68] Like Bleyer, Siebert used what he called the "big sweep" approach.[69] He wanted to write "a comprehensive history of the First Amendment"[70] in three volumes, one for the British background, one for early America and one for developments after the Constitution.[71] Only the first book of three was published, two decades after the research was done in England. Other activities interrupted his plan.

Siebert continued to contribute research to briefs in First Amendment cases, especially ones that protected the business interests of media owners. His knowledge of press taxation was used by the newspaper attorney in *Grosjean v. American Press*,[72] an important precedent for the principle that discriminatory taxes can violate the First Amendment. Justice George Sutherland, Siebert said, "incorporated in this opinion large sections of the brief tracing the history of 'taxes on knowledge' taken from the memorandum which I had prepared."[73] The *Chicago Tribune*'s law firm contacted Siebert when Col. McCormick prompted an antitrust action by using the AP's by-laws to deny membership in the wire service to a competing daily. Siebert concluded that the First Amendment would be of little or no help on an antitrust matter, but the briefs used his accurate predictions about the harmful economic effects a ruling against AP would have on its competitors.[74] Rejecting the argument that the First Amendment protected the press from antitrust enforcement, the Supreme Court ruled in favor of the government in *Associated Press v. U.S.*[75] Siebert later wrote memoranda to help *Esquire* obtain favorable mailing rates and to assert that newspapers have a First Amendment right to operate broadcast stations.[76]

Siebert's credentials as a lawyer and journalism professor made him a logical choice for other responsibilities. He became legal counsel and secretary to the Illinois Press Association and counsel and chairman of the Law of the Press Committee of the Inland Daily Press Association.[77] He was a leader of journalism education

[68]Siebert, *supra* note 55, at 447.

[69]Hudson, *supra* note 41, at 13.

[70]Siebert, *supra* note 55, at 447.

[71]Richard A. Schwarzlose, *A Conversation with Fredrick S. Siebert*, 5 JOURNALISM HIST. 106, 106 (1978–79).

[72]297 U.S. 333 (1936).

[73]Siebert, *supra* note 55, at 448.

[74]*Id.* at 448–49.

[75]326 U.S. 1 (1945).

[76]Siebert, *supra* note 55, at 449–50.

[77]Siebert, *supra* note 7, at 10–3, 5.

organizations[78] and headed programs at two universities. In 1941 he was appointed director of the School of Journalism at Illinois. His predecessor, Lawrence W. Murphy, had worked with the Illinois Press Association to establish an independent journalism program at the university, but he became discouraged during the Depression and, Siebert thought, had let the school stagnate.[79] In his presidential address to the American Association of Teachers of Journalism in 1932, Murphy described journalism schools as trying to make progress despite opposition within universities, skepticism from news organizations and "the carefree and unresponsive attitude of a generation of students."[80]

Siebert worked, like Willard Bleyer, to encourage scholarship, to stress the intellectual aspects of journalism education, and to have productive relationships with the media. He found that the state press association could be helpful in pressuring the university administration for funds, but could also be more involved in the school than he wanted. Industry interference around the country, he said, put pressure on some journalism schools to be too much like vocational training programs. Feeling he had done all he could after thirty years at Illinois, Siebert left for Michigan State University where he was dean of the College of Communication Arts from 1959 until 1967.[81] In 1976 he received the first Willard G. Bleyer research award from the Association for Education in Journalism. In making the presentation, Harold Nelson of the University of Wisconsin–Madison praised both Bleyer and Siebert for their contributions to education and scholarship.[82] Siebert, however, said in his diary that he made a terrible mistake in being seduced by the prestige of administration because the attraction soon faded, and he neglected the research and teaching he preferred to do. He wrote that he was, nevertheless, proud of having helped the field become more research-oriented.[83]

BIBLIOGRAPHY

Siebert's quest for status, for himself and for his field, put him in positions that made taking unconventional positions unlikely or

---

[78]*Id.* at 10–5.

[79]*Id.* at 10–6.

[80]Lawrence W. Murphy, *Professional and Nonprofessional Teaching of Journalism*, 9 JOURNALISM Q. 46, 57 (1932).

[81]Siebert, *supra* note 7, at 10–8; Hudson, *supra* note 41, at 1, 4.

[82]Harold L. Nelson, Presentation of the First Willard G. Bleyer Award 1–4 (1976) (unpublished manuscript, AEJMC Papers, State Historical Society of Wisconsin).

[83]Siebert, *supra* note 7, at 14–1. *See also* Siebert, *supra* note 55, at 448.

even hazardous. As a lawyer, a legal historian who contributed to court briefs, an important figure in journalism and professional organizations, and an academic administrator, he had reasons to be cautious, but he also had the example of Willard Bleyer's bold, principled statements. Both Bleyer and Siebert wanted to understand historical change and to find solutions for current, seemingly unresolvable media problems. They took risks and sought reforms. They did not always take the same positions, but they both practiced critical thinking. While the no-nonsense Bleyer pointed out problems and advocated social responsibility in journalism, Siebert was relatively relaxed about media practices. He did not expect mass communication to be foolproof or completely free, but he had been raised with respect for dissent and wanted to do research on the logic and societal forces behind suppression.

Siebert's early scholarship did not dispute the Holmesian view that law evolved in response to perceived necessities.[84] His 1927 *Journalism Bulletin* article, "Rights in News," was based on his undergraduate thesis, "Property Rights in News." The article described a process of "adjusting the legal principles of a century ago to modern facts and circumstances."[85] Siebert's 1928 *Journalism Quarterly* article on contempt of court and the press showed a similar interest in what he called "a very delicate balance"[86] and the "adjustment of the rights of both parties."[87] Noting that courts did not protect libel, blasphemy, obscenity and sedition, the budding lawyer wrote, "It is not contended by the most ardent supporters of the broad construction of the constitutional amendment that newspapers should be given unlimited freedom to publish articles which result in open and manifest harm to society."[88] The same article did, however, suggest that restrictions were hard to justify. Arbitrary, non-emergency contempt actions against journalists did not preserve the dignity of courts or make them more efficient, he said.[89] While recognizing "the most flagrant evils of modern sensational newspaper reporting,"[90] Siebert defended journalistic freedom by quoting Senator James

---

[84]*See* OLIVER WENDELL HOLMES JR., THE COMMON LAW 1 (Little, Brown 1923) (1881).

[85]*Theses on Journalism—Part II*, JOURNALISM BULL., June 1926, at 46; Fredrick S. Siebert, *Rights in the News*, JOURNALISM BULL., Nov. 1927, at 45.

[86]Fredrick Siebert, *Contempt of Court and the Press*, 5 JOURNALISM Q. 22, 22 (1928).

[87]*Id.* at 23.

[88]*Id.* at 22.

[89]*Id.* at 32–33.

[90]*Id.* at 33.

Reed as saying, "'Liberty of the press and liberty of speech is not the right to expose and defend the right, it is the right to advocate the wrong.'"[91]

The article's use of such sentiments may help to explain why Col. McCormick was impressed enough to invite its inexperienced author to help prepare the *Near* brief. A communication scholar who saw the attractive aspects of press freedom, Siebert regarded America's imperfect media system as better than the alternatives. Taking a worldwide perspective, his 1932 article on "International Protection of Rights in News" praised journalism being conducted by "commercial institutions of a quasi-public nature"[92] and condemned government-subsidized media because of the potential for suppression and propaganda.[93] Having experience with family financial troubles and with a successful publisher who championed press freedom and admired his research, he saw capitalistic communication enterprises as source of strength. "A truly independent and free press depends largely on its ability to furnish an unadulterated and wholesome commodity—news," he wrote. "Assured of financial stability founded on this service, it can espouse any political program or attack any of the evils of society which come to its attention."[94] Independent, thriving media, he thought, are "public service institutions" that supply the information and ideas citizens need.[95]

Journalism professors could see the press in a much less positive light in the 1930s. Some complained that the Roosevelt administration was not being treated fairly on the many editorial pages controlled by wealthy publishers. In a presidential address to the American Association of Teachers of Journalism published in *Journalism Quarterly* in 1935, Kenneth E. Olson praised the New Deal for seeking social justice and argued that the news media needed critical evaluation. Readers, he said, were being given gossip and comic strips when they needed analyses of rights and change. "The newspaper has become the voice of an institution representing stockholders interested in profits," Olson said.[96] In a 1934 article defending New Deal labor policies from publishers' attacks, Willard Bleyer argued that citizens depended on the ability of newspapers to inform the

---

[91]*Id.* at 22.

[92]Fredrick S. Siebert, *International Protection of Rights in News*, 9 JOURNALISM Q. 290, 290 (1932).

[93]*Id.* at 304.

[94]*Id.* at 290

[95]*Id.*

[96]Kenneth E. Olson, *The Newspaper in Times of Social Change*, 12 JOURNALISM Q. 9, 11 (1935).

public, a responsibility they often failed to meet because without self-regulation they were devoted to "monopolistic capitalism"[97] and self-serving propaganda.[98] "Just as the discredited *laissez-faire* individualism has brought us to the present crisis in our economic life," he said, "so unrestricted freedom of the press may prove equally disastrous to democratic government and society."[99] Bleyer commented that if the country turned toward fascism, many newspapers would "have little trouble in following such leadership."[100] Preserving freedom of the press, he maintained, would depend "not on any constitutional guarantee but on public opinion, the spirit of the people and of their government."[101]

Both Siebert and his former teacher were interested in the quality of news, but Bleyer was much more bothered by economic pressures and widespread conservative bias. In a 1935 article called "Freedom of Propaganda," Siebert responded to Bleyer and to Ross J. S. Hoffman, a New York University professor who called for government action against the "mass-production lying"[102] that occurred when "'liars and lunatics rave into 40,000,000 radios.'"[103] After saying that financially strong newspapers could be better at resisting corrupting influences than weak ones,[104] Siebert observed that "mental adjustment"[105] was necessary for economic changes and that the government itself can "flood the country with propaganda at a moment's notice."[106] Although noting that libel, sedition in wartime and obscenity were not considered protected in contemporary law,[107] he said that the founders were used to propagandists being "as free as the air"[108] and thought that legal restrictions on opinion were unwise.[109] "Under our constitutional guaranties promotion alone, no matter how noxious the objective, can never be legally outlawed," Siebert maintained. "The judicial sagacity necessary to separate the true from the false, it was felt, is beyond human powers."[110]

[97]Bleyer, *supra* note 30, at 27.
[98]*Id.* at 33.
[99]*Id.* at 32–33.
[100]*Id.* at 35.
[101]*Id.*
[102]Fredrick Seaton Siebert, *Freedom of Propaganda*, 12 JOURNALISM Q. 27, 32 (1935).
[103]*Id.*
[104]*Id.* at 34.
[105]*Id.* at 36.
[106]*Id.* at 35.
[107]*Id.* at 30.
[108]*Id.* at 35.
[109]*Id.*
[110]*Id.* at 35–36.

Siebert could see that the founders' conception of freedom was in conflict with what courts did and what society often expected. The media law textbook he published in 1934 noted that the press had a duty to inform the public adequately and accurately[111] and that "heroic"[112] battles for its freedom "are a part of the march of democracy,"[113] but said that the press "is not superior to the system of government under which it operates"[114] and has "no special privileges before the law."[115] Maintaining that the courts had not established clear standards of protection,[116] he quoted Justice Holmes to the effect that the Constitution is a "'living'"[117] document and said that his "clear and present danger" test had not been interpreted liberally enough to comply with the founders' elimination of seditious libel.[118] "There is little doubt that prosecutions for criticizing the Federal Government are illegal under the Constitution," Siebert wrote, "but the enactment of sedition and espionage acts during and following the World War render this interpretation questionable."[119] The right of a citizen to be informed, he said, competed with an individual's right to reputation and the authority of government to restrict immoral influences and "to maintain itself in times of stress."[120] Siebert thus acknowledged that a broad protection established by a nation could be reduced by various legal actions thought to be justifiable. "Only by a wise balance of social interests can any stable interpretation be attained," he wrote.[121]

Shifting and vague interpretations were a reality Siebert had to describe in his scholarship, but balancing could seem wise and therefore was hard to attack. After Pearl Harbor, he gathered a large collection of materials on the imposition of wartime censorship for his teaching and for a manuscript he wanted to publish.[122] He was, however, still trying to complete his book on English press law and was,

---

[111]FREDRICK SEATON SIEBERT, THE RIGHTS AND PRIVILEGES OF THE PRESS vii (1934).

[112]*Id.*

[113]*Id.*

[114]*Id.* at viii.

[115]*Id.*

[116]*Id.* at 11–12.

[117]*Id.* at 12.

[118]*Id.* at 11.

[119]*Id.*

[120]*Id.* at 12

[121]*Id.*

[122]Letter from Fredrick Siebert to Milton Hopwood, Office of Public Relations, Navy Department 1 (Mar. 21, 1942) (Siebert Papers, State Historical Society of Wisconsin).

perhaps, not prepared to face the kind of patriotic backlash a fault-finding effort could produce. In any case, Siebert was somewhat resigned to the reality of restraints. Knowing that First Amendment absolutism was rejected by the government officials the press was supposed to be free to challenge, he was often content merely to challenge the logic and operation of press controls.

In 1948, in a chapter he wrote for a collection of essays on the mass media, Siebert diagnosed some ills in communication law, but lacked precise cures. He thought that some government-enforced solution might be found for the "frequently disgraceful" sensational coverage of crime and courts.[123] Libel cases were slow and complex, he said, and did not provide adequate remedies for the injured or prevent harassment of the media by the unscrupulous.[124] His answer was to throw out the libel precedents dating back to the seventeenth century and to find "a new remedy which will fit American conditions and American needs."[125] He also criticized the enforcement of obscenity and sedition statutes.[126] Choosing the "wisdom" of history over expedient decisions,[127] Siebert objected to regulatory actions that would affect the marketplace of ideas.[128] He offered the "tentative"[129] conclusion that government should "keep its hands off information content."[130] While suspicious of the motives of the decision makers, he said that some business rules[131] and some government secrecy are necessary.[132] Even in a democracy, he warned, officials were "still likely to be more interested in maintaining their official position than in protecting the rights of the people or even promoting the 'interests of society.'"[133] Siebert nevertheless stated that government should be able to facilitate existing and new media and that he had "no fundamental objection" to government having its own broadcast stations to reach the public directly even if they were dull and wasteful.[134]

---

[123]Fred S. Siebert, *Communications and Government*, *in* COMMUNICATIONS IN MODERN SOCIETY 10 (Wilbur Schramm ed., 1948).

[124]*Id.*

[125]*Id.* at 11.

[126]*Id.* at 9.

[127]*Id.* at 12.

[128]*Id.* at 11–12.

[129]*Id.* at 14.

[130]*Id.*

[131]*Id.* at 12.

[132]*Id.* at 13.

[133]*Id.* at 11.

[134]*Id.* at 14.

The foundation of Siebert's laissez-faire thinking was exhibited in his book *Freedom of the Press in England 1476–1776: The Rise and Decline of Government Control*, which was published in 1952. A detailed, well-organized account of the absurdities, injustices and futilities of government trying to protect itself with suppression, the book begins by observing that capitalism, democracy and press freedom were "inextricably interrelated" and arose together.[135] The Introduction says that by the late eighteenth century a branch of Anglo-American thought associated with Jefferson and others, one that became generally accepted in the United States, contended that "a government could not restrict the right to speak and to print, even to save itself from destruction."[136] He attributed the position to the development of popular sovereignty, publishers' insistence on being unhampered as they pursued profit, and philosophical principles associated with freedom of thought.[137] He noted, however, that no one's theory of press freedom endorsed complete liberty and that the restrictions could be nebulous.[138] "All agree that some forms of restraint are necessary and that the government has a legitimate function to define the limitations," he wrote.[139] Siebert said that everyone believed that "it is the function of government to protect private reputations, to control to some unspecified degree the distribution of obscene matter, and to regulate to a still more vague degree publications which undermine the basic structure of organized society."[140]

Siebert looked for patterns in the development and decline of general constitutional principles in England and the United States. Using his historical knowledge, he wrote two theory statements in the Introduction. Proposition I asserted: "The extent of government control of the press depends on the nature of the relationship of the government to those subject to the government."[141] A more accountable political system, he reasoned, would have more liberty of the press.[142] Proposition II maintained: "The area of freedom contracts

[135]SIEBERT, *supra* note 67, at vi.

[136]*Id.* at 7.

[137]*Id.* at 7–9.

[138]*Id.* at 9.

[139]*Id.*

[140]*Id.* In his acknowledgments, Siebert wrote, "Prof. Zechariah Chafee, Jr., of Harvard Law School, made extremely useful comments on the manuscript." *Id.* at viii. At the same time, Chafee was writing a paper that described expression as sometimes subordinated to societal interests, the common law and the powers of Congress. "It is true that the First Amendment does not mention any limitations," he wrote. "It just says 'Congress shall pass no law. … ' Yet the limitations are there just the same." ZECHARIAH CHAFEE, JR., THE BLESSINGS OF LIBERTY 282 (1956).

[141]SIEBERT, *supra* note 67, at 10.

[142]*Id.*

and the enforcement of restraints increases as the stresses on the stability of the government and of the structure of society increase."[143] The First Amendment absolutism of the founders, Siebert explained, was "modified in operation"[144] in accordance with Proposition II as the nation fought wars and the courts fashioned unclear standards for allowable expression.[145] "The safety of the state is still a criterion for measuring the amount of freedom allotted to the press," he wrote.[146]

Siebert's theory statements were not novel. Proposition I is little more than a long-held structural rationale of civil libertarians that popular sovereignty and the people's rights are logically linked. Proposition II simply observed that public officials react to perceived threats by silencing them. Later scholars, however, were interested enough by the propositions to try to refine and expand Siebert's thinking.[147] Siebert himself did not expect the attention his Introduction received. "In a way that kind of surprises me," Siebert said later. "I didn't think it was that good."[148]

Whatever the shortcomings may be, the Introduction sums up the story Siebert constructed from an abundance of archival material. He was venturing into a social science understanding of law. The British press prior to the American Revolution, Siebert wrote, "was an integrated part of the entire social organism affecting and being affected by the society of which it is a part."[149] He had a similar perspective on press freedom in the United States. The Introduction to *Four Theories of the Press*, a book of essays by Siebert and his colleagues Theodore Peterson and Wilbur Schramm, holds that "the press always takes on the form and coloration of the social and political structures within which it operates."[150]

Siebert outlined the ideas for *Four Theories of the Press* in a 1953 speech accepting the Kappa Tau Alpha research award for his book on England. He described the first theory, authoritarian, as supporting government power and as breaking down in England with the

[143]*Id.*

[144]*Id.* at 11.

[145]*Id.* at 11–12.

[146]*Id.* at 11.

[147]*See* Jeffery A. Smith, *Further Steps Toward a Theory of Press Control*, 8 JOURNALISM HIST. 93 (1981).

[148]Schwarzlose, *supra* note 71, at 108.

[149]SIEBERT, *supra* note 67, at vi.

[150]FRED S. SIEBERT ET. AL., FOUR THEORIES OF THE PRESS: THE AUTHORITARIAN, LIBERTARIAN, SOCIAL RESPONSIBILITY AND SOVIET COMMUNIST CONCEPTS OF WHAT THE PRESS SHOULD BE AND DO 1 (1956).

growth of political and economic freedom.[151] Libertarian theory made the press independent of public officials and, he declared in an echo of Col. McCormick, able to provide "that check on government which no government itself can provide."[152] Stating a precept later recognized in *New York Times v. Sullivan*,[153] Siebert said libertarian theory regarded the news media as constitutionally protected "in exposing, even erroneously and viciously, those activities especially of government, which affected the public welfare."[154] Communist theory, he wrote dismissively, distrusted the "fickle" masses and expected state-owned media to convey pre-determined truths determined by party ideology.[155] Without mentioning Bleyer or others he knew, he said that the fourth theory, social responsibility, had emerged by the mid-1920s and had questioned the ability of privately owned media to inform the public. Defending powerful news organizations, Siebert said that "enlightened" media managers took their public service responsibilities seriously and that big businesses still depended on meeting the needs and wishes of their customers.[156]

Siebert's talk, which appeared in *Vital Speeches*, ended with a historical review of the approach he favored with some reservations, libertarian theory. He said that libertarian principles on press freedom were accepted in the state and federal constitutions and he mentioned the Federalist argument that a guarantee was not needed because the government was not given any power over journalists.[157] Except for some "aberrations," Siebert said, "the American system of uncontrolled public discussion of controversial public issues expanded throughout the 19th century."[158] In the twentieth century, he wrote, "Congress evidently felt it had powers to place restraints on the mass media particularly in a state of war" and, therefore, the courts grappled unsatisfactorily with defining the limits of press freedom.[159] Referring to Cold War fears and conformism, he concluded: "In spite of what might appear to be current set-backs, I am confident on the basis of historical perspective that we can resolve this issue."[160]

---

[151]Fredrick S. Siebert, *The Historical Pattern of Press Freedom*, 19 VITAL SPEECHES 659, 659–60 (1953).
[152]*Id.* at 660.
[153]376 U.S. 254 (1964).
[154]Siebert, *supra* note 151, at 660.
[155]*Id.*
[156]*Id.* at 660–61.
[157]*Id.* at 661.
[158]*Id.*
[159]*Id.* at 662.
[160]*Id.*

In failing to take a more forthright stand for freedom of expression, Siebert might have been wary of condemning the nation's suppressive mood or of challenging the doubts about democratic communication that intellectuals had been expressing for decades. Apparently influenced by the outlook of Walter Lippmann and others, Willard Bleyer made known his qualms about the abilities of citizens to do the information processing necessary for political decisions. In an article published in 1926, he worried that emotions affected public opinion and that intolerance jeopardized press freedom.[161] Siebert wrote in *Four Theories of the Press* that the pure libertarian theories of the founders had been adjusted in various, vague ways to modern realities. In reviewing the laws affecting the media, he objected to imprecise standards, but looked for a positive perspective. He described libertarian theory as "muddling through"[162] with "its flexibility, its adaptability to change, and above all its confidence in its ability to advance the interests and welfare of human beings by continuing to place its trust in individual self-direction."[163]

The restrictions Siebert wrote about in *Four Theories of the Press* could, of course, limit "self-direction" in significant ways. Thomas I. Emerson later took a more confident "full protection" approach to traditional libertarian theory when he examined the history of press freedom and the incoherent First Amendment doctrines of the twentieth century. "This is to say that expression must be protected against government curtailment at all points, even where the results of expression may appear to be in conflict with other social interests the government is charged with safeguarding," Emerson wrote in 1970.[164]

By 1970 the nation's political climate had changed and the press was being subjected to more scrutiny. That year, Siebert was asked about the disparagement news organizations were receiving from the Nixon administration. He replied that the accusations went too far, but kept the media "on their toes." He said that journalism educators should be in the forefront of press criticism. "I think this new generation of people in journalism schools are more willing to be critical than were the previous generation, when they were trying to sell themselves to the profession," he told an oral history interviewer, "so you've got a better base from which to operate."[165] Exposing the faults of the media, of

[161]Willard Grosvenor Bleyer, *The Press and Public Opinion in International Relations*, JOURNALISM BULL., June 1926, at 7, 19.

[162]SIEBERT ET. AL., *supra* note 150, at 67.

[163]*Id.* at 71.

[164]THOMAS I. EMERSON, THE SYSTEM OF FREEDOM OF EXPRESSION 17 (1970).

[165]Hudson, *supra* note 41, at 10.

course, did not mean endorsing government controls. Discussing his own scholarship with an interviewer in 1978, Siebert said that the willingness of journalists to fight for press freedom needed to be considered. "It doesn't come by itself," he said.[166]

Three years before his death in 1982, Fred Siebert recounted the events of his career in a *Journalism Quarterly* article that dwelled on his pleasure in researching the roguish libertine John Wilkes who championed press freedom in England.[167] The article ended with the sentence: "By now it should be apparent that the First Amendment and I have had a life-long love affair."[168] Like any romantic relationship, the connection could be complicated by uncertainties and concrete concerns. The First Amendment of Siebert's lifetime, lacking its attachment to the founders' absolutism, was unmoored in a sea of perplexing interpretations and interposing expectations. He could not secure liberty of the press to what he saw as its original meaning, but could describe damage the concept sustained, contractions from suppression and dishonor from irresponsible journalism. A believer in the broadest possible protection, he had to watch the First Amendment being bent by beliefs about prudence and propriety and defaced by unprofessional practices. As the ever-realistic James Madison understood, any notion that freedom of expression would always remain rigid and pristine was a fantasy, but the written guarantee has not been as fragile or as futile as he might have feared. Its beauty remains in the eyes of its beholders as it begins another century of existence.

[166]Schwarzlose, *supra* note 71, at 123.
[167]Siebert, *supra* note 55, at 448.
[168]*Id.* at 450.

7 COMM. L. & POL'Y 401–430 (2002)

AN APOLOGIA TO RADICAL DISSENT AND A SUPREME COURT TEST TO PROTECT IT

SUSAN DENTE ROSS*

Some framers of the Constitution of the United States, scholars and Supreme Court justices have argued that protection and encouragement of democratic deliberation are at the core purpose of the First Amendment. Most of these individuals would, nevertheless, exclude radical political dissent from constitutional protection. They seem to disagree with Thomas Jefferson, who believed in the salutary effects of revolutionary speech and even the occasional revolution. Government action targeting terrorist speech and association extends from this reasoning. This article argues that extreme political speech has benefit to society. Building on a varied body of First Amendment opinions, the author proposes a five-part test to better protect the radical speech vital to self-government and the search for truth.

> You make men love their government and their country by giving them the kind of government and the kind of country that inspire respect and love: a country that is free and unafraid, that lets the discontented talk in order to learn the causes for their discontent and end those causes, that refuses to impel men to spy on their neighbors, that protects its citizens vigorously from harmful acts while it leaves the remedies for objectionable ideas to counter-argument and time.[1]

So wrote Harvard Law Professor Zechariah Chafee in 1941, referring specifically to the shadow of censorship cast over the nation in the years after World War I. His treatise on *Free Speech in the United*

---

*Associate Professor, Edward R. Murrow School of Communication, Washington State University.

[1]ZECHARIAH CHAFEE, JR., FREE SPEECH IN THE UNITED STATES 565 (2d ed. 1942).

States recognized a recurrent pattern of censorship in England and throughout the history of the United States. Others have noted that fear motivates governments generally to protect free speech only erratically. Thus, Frederick S. Siebert, who examined the English history of government censorship or advancement of speech, found that "freedom contracts and the enforcement of restraints increases as the stresses on the stability of the government and of the structure of society increase."[2] Thus, Siebert concluded, "How much freedom we shall enjoy will depend on how widespread are the threats and the feeling of insecurity and instability."[3]

As the ultimate guardian of free speech in this country, the Supreme Court of the United States could interpret the First Amendment to the Constitution to counterbalance the natural tendency of government to constrict civil liberties. This role of the Court is so fundamental that even at the height of World War II, Justice Robert H. Jackson would concur with the Court's decision to strike down regulation of union organizers and assert:

> The very purpose of the First Amendment is to foreclose public authority from assuming a guardianship of the public mind through regulating the press, speech, and religion. In this field every person must be his own watchman for truth, because the forefathers did not trust any government to separate the true from the false for us.[4]

In this view, a primary function of the Supreme Court would be to strive to curb the tendency of government to over-regulate. Accordingly, the Court's decisions on dissident speech or government limitations upon association and expression should be animated not by fear of the unknown but by the principle that citizens in a democratic state must be encouraged to speak openly and critically about government and public affairs in order to discharge the rights and duties of citizenship.

Yet, despite nods to the vital role uninhibited debate plays in democratic self-governance, the Court has not consistently advanced a broad presumption against government action that encourages orthodoxy or discourages open discussion. Instead, as legal historian

---

[2]FREDERICK S. SIEBERT, FREEDOM OF THE PRESS IN ENGLAND 1476–1776: THE RISE AND DECLINE OF GOVERNMENT CONTROL 10 (1952). *See also* MARGARET A. BLANCHARD, REVOLUTIONARY SPARKS viii–ix (1992) (calling the tendency to censor the "urge toward conformity").

[3]SIEBERT, *supra* note 2, at 13.

[4]Thomas v. Collins, 323 U.S. 516, 545 (1944) (Jackson, J., concurring).

Margaret Blanchard noted, "The United States has lurched from periods when revolutionary ideas were soundly and, at times, violently repressed to times when the nation was rocked by the raucousness of uninhibited discussion."[5] Lee Bollinger suggested that such vacillations in free speech protection are the logical result of a judiciary "left largely adrift on a sea of possible interpretations of the First Amendment"[6] and asked to "giv[e] content" to an inchoate and malleable Constitution.[7]

The absence of a strong judicial presumption in favor of radical discussion and dissent provides fertile ground for erosion of liberty in times of fear and disquiet. These are such times. This article, therefore, crafts a test by which the Supreme Court could increase the consistency and vigor of protection for dissent.

Some would argue that tests do not protect speech. Indeed, Judge Learned Hand once said,

> I often wonder whether we do not rest our hopes too much upon constitutions, upon laws and upon courts. These are false hopes; believe me, these are false hopes. Liberty lies in the hearts of men and women; when it dies there, no constitution, no law, no court can save it. ... While it lies there, it needs no constitution, no law, no court to save it.[8]

Indeed, the essence of free speech protections lies in a profound national commitment to the intrinsic and the instrumental, the personal and the social values of this fundamental freedom. This commitment, according to Blanchard, represents "the conscience of the nation"[9] and assures the moral independence and sovereignty of the people.[10]

While a new Supreme Court test to scrutinize government infringements on radical dissent is not sufficient to safeguard this speech, it is not idle to posit such a test. A rigorous test may provide the Court with a helpful justification for unpopular rulings, or it may become the vessel into which justices pour their robust and eloquent commitment to freedom of expression.

---

[5]BLANCHARD, *supra* note 2, at 489.

[6]LEE BOLLINGER, THE TOLERANT SOCIETY 6 (1986).

[7]*Id.* at 225.

[8]Judge Learned Hand, *The Spirit of Liberty, in* OUR NATION'S ARCHIVE: THE HISTORY OF THE UNITED STATES IN DOCUMENTS (Erik Bruun and Jay Crosby eds., 1999) (speech presented in New York City, 1944).

[9]BLANCHARD, *supra* note 2, at 489.

[10]*See* DAVID A.J. RICHARDS, TOLERATION AND THE CONSTITUTION 85, 101 (1986). *See generally* RONALD DWORKIN, FREEDOM'S LAW: THE MORAL READING OF THE AMERICAN CONSTITUTION (1996).

The following section of this article begins with summary discussions of the nature of liberty and of suppression and the value of radical dissent. The Supreme Court's treatment of dissent then is explored through two distinct areas of case law. The author next proposes a test that might better protect the role of dissent in America. The article concludes by examining the implications of the proposed doctrine on the extent and diversity of open public debate in the United States today.

LIBERTY, SUPRESSION & RADICAL DISSENT

Under democratic theory, fear of government censorship arises from the practical need of citizens to be free to discuss the foibles of their representatives. This view arises from a historical reading of the First Amendment as uniquely concerned with the processes of democratic self-governance.[11] A more overarching solicitude for freedom from government censorship envisions a wide-open and robust exchange of ideas to be essential to both individual and societal interests.[12] Thus, Professor Chafee repeatedly wrote:

> One of the most important purposes of society and government is the discovery and spread of truth on subjects of general concern. This is possible only through absolutely unlimited discussion, for ... once force is thrown into the argument, it becomes a matter of chance whether it is thrown on the false side or the true, and truth loses all its natural advantage in the contest.[13]

Political philosophers and legal scholars for centuries have asserted that censorship erodes the search for truth and the vitality of accepted wisdom.[14] In 1664, John Stuart Mill noted that "however

[11]*See, e.g.*, ALEXANDER MEIKLEJOHN, FREE SPEECH AND ITS RELATION TO SELF-GOVERNMENT (1948); HARRY KALVEN, JR., A WORTHY TRADITION: FREEDOM OF SPEECH IN AMERICA (1988); Robert H. Bork, *Neutral Principles and Some First Amendment Problems*, 47 IND. LAW J. 1 (1971); Harry Kalven, Jr., *The* New York Times *Case: A Note on "The Central Meaning of the First Amendment,"* 1964 SUP. CT. REV. 191.

[12]*See* THOMAS I. EMERSON, THE SYSTEM OF FREEDOM OF EXPRESSION 6–7 (1970) (enumerating four social and personal values served by free expression).

[13]ZECHARIAH CHAFEE, FREEDOM OF SPEECH 34 (1920) and 31 (1941); Zechariah Chafee, *Freedom of Speech in War Time*, 32 HARV. L. REV. 932, 956–57 (1919); Zechariah Chafee, *Freedom of Speech*, 17 NEW REPUBLIC 66, 67 (1918).

[14]*See, e.g.*, EMERSON, *supra* note 12, at 51 (1970) ("Even if we consider freedom of expression an absolute value ... nevertheless it is important that it remain open to challenge. Otherwise it becomes a 'dead dogma,' ill- understood, lacking in vitality, and vulnerable to erosion or full-scale attack."); JOHN STUART MILL, ON LIBERTY 97,

true [an opinion] may be, if it is not fully, frequently, and fearlessly discussed, it will be held as a dead dogma, not a living truth. ... [Even if] the received opinion [is] true, a conflict with the opposite error is essential to a clear apprehension and deep feeling of its truth."[15] According to this view, a proper government must advance—not stifle—diverse and extreme debate to assure that truths do not wither and die. Indeed, in 1794 James Madison noted a significant distinction between the British crown and the republican form of government adopted by the new nation: In the United States "the censorial power [is] in the people over the Government, and not in the Government over the people."[16] Similarly, in 1950 Justice Hugo Black wrote:

> [T]he postulate of the First Amendment is that our free institutions can be maintained without proscribing or penalizing political belief, speech, press, assembly, or party affiliation. This is a far bolder philosophy than despotic rulers can afford to follow. It is the heart of the system on which our freedom depends.[17]

But in documenting the history of royal censorship in England that predated the founding of the United States and provided a major impetus for the Bill of Rights, Siebert argued that the urge to censor "is true for all types of governments."[18] Thus, advocates of the democratic system must watch jealously over the actions of government. This is particularly true, Cass Sunstein noted, because "government is rightly distrusted when it is regulating speech that might harm its own interests; and when the speech at issue is political, its own interests are almost always at stake."[19] Indeed, as Justice William O. Douglas wrote in 1971, government's "eternal temptation ... has

108 (Gertrude Himmelfarb ed., Penguin Books 1985) (1859); JOHN MILTON, AREOPAGITICA, A SPEECH OF MR. JOHN MILTON FOR THE LIBERTY OF UNLICENC'D PRINTING, TO THE PARLIAMENT OF ENGLAND (J.C. Suffolk ed., 1968) (1644). Note, however, that a Lexis-Nexis search of all Supreme Court opinions found no references to "dead dogma."

[15]JOHN STUART MILL, *supra* note 14, at 34.

[16]4 ANNALS OF CONG. 934 (1794), *quoted in* New York Times v. Sullivan, 376 U.S. 254, 275 (1964). *But see* BLANCHARD, *supra* note 2, at xii; LEONARD W. LEVY, LEGACY OF SUPPRESSION 227 (1960) (noting that the framers understood that "constitutional protections of rights meant little during times of popular hysteria.").

[17]Amer. Communications Ass'n v. Douds, 339 U.S. 382, 452–453 (1950) (Black, J., dissenting) (affirming national rule requiring union organizers to swear they have no Communist affiliations).

[18]SIEBERT, *supra* note 2, at 10–11.

[19]CASS R. SUNSTEIN, DEMOCRACY AND THE PROBLEM OF FREE SPEECH 134 (1995).

been to arrest the speaker rather than to correct the conditions about which he complains."[20]

Siebert cautioned against sweeping assumptions about democratic correctives to government censorship.[21] Oftentimes, neither citizens nor the judiciary can access the necessary information to ably evaluate the merit of government's justifications for censorial actions. As a consequence, the high court has recognized that government's tendency to overstate the potential injuries of speech may at times go unchecked.[22] In 1972, for example, Justice Douglas wrote, "The secrecy stamp is the officials' tool of suppression, and it has been used to withhold information which in 99½% of the cases would present no danger to national security."[23] It has been said that eternal vigilance is the price of liberty;[24] it also may be said that eternal vigilance must be the corrective to government suppression. As Chafee noted, "We must do more than remove the discouragements to open discussion. We must exert ourselves to supply active encouragements"[25] to truly free speech.

History, writ long or short, demonstrates that the Supreme Court has failed to be eternally vigilant of free speech rights. Particularly during times of national or international strain, the Court has not consistently removed discouragements or provided active encouragements to radical debate and dissent. The Court's well-established record of defining, and then excluding from the First Amendment ambit, any speech that has a "bad tendency," or that presents a "clear and present danger," or that "incites"[26] is one source of problems. As Justice Douglas noted:

---

[20]Younger v. Harris, 401 U.S. 37, 65 (1971) (Douglas, J., dissenting).

[21]SUNSTEIN, *supra* note 19. *See also* LEVY, *supra* note 16, at 233.

[22]*See, e.g.,* New York Times v. United States, 403 U.S. 713, 744 (1971).

[23]Gravel v. United States, 408 U.S. 606, 642 (1972) (Douglas, J., dissenting) (rejecting congressional immunity to the aide of a senator charged with disclosing classified Pentagon documents).

[24]*See, e.g.,* Tom Nadeau, *The Trouble with Technology*, OS OPINION, May 13, 2002, *at* http://www.paulmartinart.com/EternalVigilance.html (attributing the statement to Thomas Jefferson). *But see* John Philpot Curran, *Speech Upon the Right of Election, 1790*, BARTLETT'S FAMILIAR QUOTATIONS (J. Bartlett & J. Kaplan eds, 16th ed., 1992).

[25]CHAFEE, *supra* note 1, at 559.

[26]*See, e.g.,* the anti-slavery cases (NAACP v. Claiborne Hardware, 458 U.S. 886 (1982); Elfbrandt v. Russell, 384 U.S. 11 (1966); NAACP v. Alabama 357 U.S. 449 (1958)); the Espionage Act cases (Schenck v. United States, 249 U.S. 47 (1919); Frohwerk v. United States, 249 U.S. 204 (1919); Debs v. United States, 249 U.S. 211 (1919); Abrams v. United States, 250 U.S. 616 (1919)); the criminal syndicalism case (Whitney v. California, 274 U.S. 357 (1927)); the Smith Act cases (Communist Party of the United States v. Subversive Activities Control Board, 367 U.S. 1 (1961); Den-

> The Court has not always been consistent in its protection of ... First Amendment rights and has sometimes allowed a government interest to override the absolutes of the First Amendment. For example, under the banner of the "clear and present danger" test, and later under the influence of the "balancing" formula, the Court has permitted men to be penalized not for any harmful conduct but solely for holding unpopular beliefs.[27]

Despite the Supreme Court's frequently lofty and eloquent rhetoric supporting freedom of speech, the Court has failed to develop the theoretical foundation for the freedom from government-induced orthodoxy necessary to fully protect fundamental liberties. The Court itself has described its jurisprudence in this area as "thousands of pages of confusing formulas, refined reasonings, and puzzling holdings that touch on the same suspicions and fears about citizenship and loyalty."[28] A review of Supreme Court decisions indicates that some justices believe the Court has not fully articulated—and hence not fully protected—the broad value of wide-ranging and robust dissent.[29]

Recognizing its checkered record in this domain, the Supreme Court in 1969 reshaped its definition of unprotected speech to target only incitement.[30] But, like its predecessors, the incitement test enunciated in *Brandenburg v. Ohio* has failed consistently to protect unpopular radical dissent.[31] Indeed, even when applying this most

---

nis v. United States, 341 U.S. 494 (1951)); and the anti-terrorism case (Reno v. American Arab Anti-Discrimination Committee 525 U.S. 471 (1999)).

[27]Branzburg v. Hayes, 408 U.S. 665, 716–717 (1972) (Douglas, J., dissenting).

[28]Baird v. State Bar of Arizona, 401 U.S. 1, 4 (1971).

[29]*See, e.g.*, Communist Party of Indiana v. Whitcomb, 414 U.S. 441, 447 (1974); Branzburg v. Hayes, 408 U.S. 665, 715 (1972) (Douglas, J., dissenting); Kleindienst v. Mandel, 408 U.S. 753, 773, 780 (1972) (Douglas, J., dissenting); Brandenburg v. Ohio, 395 U.S. 444 (1969); Stanley v. Georgia, 394 U.S. 557, 564 (1969); Lamont v. Postmaster General, 381 U.S. 301, 308 (1965) (Brennan, J., concurring); New York Times Co. v. Sullivan, 376 U.S. 254, 270 (1964); NAACP v. Button, 371 U.S. 415, 438 (1963); Thomas v. Collins, 323 U.S. 516, 545 (1945) (Jackson, J., concurring); Whitney v. California, 274 U.S. 357, 375, 377 (1927) (Brandeis, J., concurring).

[30]Brandenburg v. Ohio, 395 U.S. 444 (1969) (to warrant government action, the targeted speech must be intended to and likely to incite imminent lawlessness).

[31]*See, e.g.*, Lorillard Tobacco v. Reilly, 533 U.S. 525, 579 (2001) (Thomas, J., concurring) (striking state regulation of tobacco as violating First Amendment and citing *Brandenburg* to establish that government may regulate speech that *solicits* as well as incites crime); Hurley v. Irish-American Gay, Lesbian & Bisexual Group, 515 U.S. 557, 574 (1995) (holding Hurley's First Amendment freedom of association prevents government-forced inclusion of gay/lesbian group in parade and citing *Brandenburg* as supporting claim that First Amendment protects hurtful and misguided speech); Texas v. Johnson, 491 U.S. 397, 418 (1989) (protecting flag burning as protected political expression under the First Amendment and explaining *Brandenburg* to hold that even "concepts virtually sacred to our Nation" will not go

speech-protective test, the Supreme Court alternately has asserted the paramount importance of open debate about political issues or excluded certain radical political ideas from the sphere of First Amendment protection. The Court also has confined its most exuberant support for an active battle of ideas to certain privileged groups or locales (especially schools and universities).[32]

Many years ago, Professor Chafee repudiated the Court's reliance on the concept of indirect causation expressed in this approach to unpopular speech. Chafee wrote that any system predicated upon government itself determining whether "the state can punish all words [that] have some tendency, however remote, to bring about acts in violation of law, or only words [that] directly incite to acts in violation of law"[33] would lead inevitably to erosion of free speech. This study suggests the Court's stunted conception of impermissible government orthodoxy undercuts the possible role of free speech in democratic self-governance, the search for truth, the pursuit of self-fulfillment and the oversight of government.[34] Finally, the Supreme Court's selective articulation of the paramount value of dissent undermines personal liberty and throws wide the doors to repressive government actions in times of national uncertainty or stress.

---

unchallenged); United States v. Abel, 469 U.S. 45, 48 (1984) (allowing into evidence testimony alleging gang membership of prison defense witness and distinguishing *Brandenburg* on grounds that while conviction may not rest on mere association, such information may be probative of witness bias); NAACP v. Claiborne Hardware, 458 U.S. 886, 927 (1982) (applying *Brandenburg* to hold that First Amendment prohibits punishment of black boycotters for business damages caused by their overt threats or physical violence); Kleindienst v. Mandel, 408 U.S. 753, 780 (1982) (Douglas, J., dissenting) (applying *Brandenburg* to establish "that government has no legitimate interest in stopping the flow of ideas"); Central Hudson Gas & Elec. Corp. v. Public Ser. Comm'n, 447 U.S. 557, 596 (Rehnquist, J., dissenting) (1980) (arguing that obscenity and broadcast indecency may be regulated without meeting the clear and present danger or the incitement test of *Brandenburg*); Carey v. Population Services Int'l, 431 U.S. 678, 701 (1977) (explaining that *Brandenburg* incitement standard does not permit government ban on advertisements for "entirely legal" contraceptive products); Eisenstadt v. Baird, 405 U.S. 438, 459 (1972) (Douglas, J., concurring) (applying *Brandenburg* to protect persuasion to unwise or immoral action); Law Students Civil Rights Research Council v. Wadmond, 401 U.S. 154, 183 (1971) (Black, J., dissenting) (explaining *Brandenburg* to hold "that association with a group to advocate violence cannot be punished consistently with the First Amendment").

[32] *See infra* notes 64–71 and accompanying text.

[33] CHAFEE, *supra* note 1, at 23.

[34] *See generally* EMERSON, *supra* note 12.

THE NATURE OF LIBERTY

In 1927, Justice Louis Brandeis wrote, "Those who won our independence ... valued liberty both as an end and as a means."[35] Liberty, in this view, is both an instrument for social good and a fundamental right inherently worthy of societal (read governmental) protection. At mid-century, Professor Chafee expressed the popular instrumentalist view of America's commitment to freedom of speech: the First Amendment is "a declaration of national policy in favor of the public discussion of all public questions."[36] He suggested the struggle to define the proper degree of government constraint of free speech is, at base, a struggle between two competing views of government: government as master or government as servant.[37] Even the more speech-protective, classic Millian view of government as servant,[38] however, fails clearly to delineate the extent of personal freedoms or the boundaries of government power.

Other functionalist approaches value free speech as a corrective to the aggregation of power to a small elite,[39] or consider dissent to be an important expression of diversity in a pluralist society,[40] a social catharsis and a purgative.[41] Ronald Dworkin, however, argues that liberty of speech may never properly be viewed as a national policy initiative. Rather, freedom of speech arises directly and necessarily from natural law.[42] According to natural law, freedom of beliefs and their expression are an innate trait of human liberty essential to self-awareness and realization. As such, free speech is not the legitimate domain of government action.

The divergent approaches to understanding and protecting liberty reflect and perpetuate the malleability of the concept. The American conception of fundamental rights and liberties is not static but or-

---

[35]Whitney v. California, 274 U.S. 357, 372 (Brandeis, J., concurring).

[36]CHAFEE, *supra* note 1, at 6.

[37]*Id.* at 22.

[38]*See* JOHN STUART MILL, ON LIBERTY (C.V. Shields ed., 1956) (1859).

[39]*See* O.M. FISS, THE IRONY OF FREE SPEECH (1996); SUNSTEIN, *supra* note 19; Owen M. Fiss, *Why the State?* 100 HARV. L. REV. 781 (1987); O.M. Fiss, *Free Speech and Social Structure,* 71 IOWA L. REV. 1405 (1986).

[40]*See, e.g.,* STEVEN SHIFFRIN, DEMOCRACY, FREE SPEECH, AND ROMANCE (1990).

[41]*See,* Vincent Blasi, *The Pathological Perspective and the First Amendment,* 85 COLUM. L. REV. 449 (1985); Vincent Blasi, *The Checking Value in First Amendment Theory*, 1977 AMER. BAR FOUND. RES. J. 523.

[42]*See* RONALD DWORKIN, TAKING RIGHTS SERIOUSLY (1977); RONALD DWORKIN, A MATTER OF PRINCIPLE (1985); RONALD DWORKIN, FREEDOM'S LAW, THE MORAL READING OF THE AMERICAN CONSTITUTION (1996).

ganic.[43] While grounded in history and precedent, the American concept of freedom is also the product of changing social mores, scientific knowledge and economic and political concerns. The nature of liberty is inextricably tied to time and place, to history and vision, to values and fears. "Its significance," Professor Chafee wrote, is " ... the endless expression of a civilization."[44]

This fluidity of meaning is a two-edged sword. The indeterminacy offers the promise of expanding liberties in response to improved understanding of the world and our place in it. It also holds the threat of contracting freedoms in reaction to real, imagined or illusory fears. Thus, while it is both intriguing and instructive to examine a historical conception of liberty, such an exploration is not sufficient. The meaning of liberty and the American realization of that liberty are contextual. Liberty is daily enacted through the actions of government and, especially, the decisions of the Supreme Court.

THE NATURE OF SUPPRESSION

It is human nature to believe in one's own views and to hold assiduously to their correctness. As Justice Oliver Wendell Holmes wrote, "Persecution for the expression of opinions seems to me perfectly logical. If you have no doubt of your premises or your power and want a certain result with all your heart, you naturally express your wishes in law and sweep away all opposition."[45] Suppression is natural, even inevitable. Individuals, societies or elected representatives find it difficult to recognize, understand and advance ideas with which they disagree. The dangerous consequence is, as Henry Schofield once noted:

> ... that men will be fined and imprisoned, under the guise of being punished for their bad motives, or bad intent and ends, simply because the powers that be do not agree with their opinions, and spokesmen of minorities may be terrorized and silenced when they are most needed by the community and most useful to it, and when they stand most in need of the protection of the law against a hostile, arrogant majority.[46]

---

[43]*See*, Gompers v. United States, 233 U.S. 604, 610 (1914). *See also* LEONARD W. LEVY, ORIGINAL INTENT AND THE FRAMER'S CONSTITUTION xii (1988); SIEBERT, *supra* note 2, at 10.

[44]CHAFEE, *supra* note 1, at 29.

[45]Abrams v. United States, 250 U.S. 616, 630 (1919) (Holmes, J., dissenting).

[46]Henry Schofield, *Freedom of the Press in the United States*, *in* ESSAYS ON CONSTITUTIONAL LAW & EQUITY 11 (1914), *quoted in* CHAFEE, *supra* note 1, at 28.

Popular ideas need no protection, but when people voice unpopular ideas, commitment to liberty is strained.[47]

Siebert correlated the tendency of government to enact and enforce speech repressive laws with the insecurity of the regime. "It is axiomatic," Siebert wrote, "that government does not exert itself in its own protection unless it is attacked or believes itself seriously threatened."[48] Siebert expressed faith that liberty expands when threats dissipate, but this need not necessarily be true. While governments may move aggressively to limit liberties during periods of instability and uncertainty, it need not follow that repressive laws will be repealed when threats to national security abate. The regulatory pendulum need not be perfectly self-righting. Therefore, the shadow of oppression may well extend beyond the period of overt government concern.

THE VALUE OF RADICAL IDEAS

Radical ideas, like all ideas, have unique inherent worth. The mere existence of extreme ideas expands the realm of the imaginable and reshapes the known. Extremist[49] views push outward the boundaries of perceived reality and make less radical ideas appear more mainstream.[50] Radical expression also often represents a broader, though perhaps more moderate, body of discontent. As Chafee recognized:

> [T]he pertinacious orators and writers who get hauled up are merely extremist spokesmen for a mass of more thoughtful and more retiring men and women, who share in varying degrees the same critical attitude toward prevailing policies and institutions. When you put the hotheads in jail, these cooler people do not get arrested—they just keep quiet. And so we lose things they could tell us, which would be very advantageous for the future course of the nation.[51]

---

[47]CHAFEE, *supra* note 1, at 4.

[48]SIEBERT, *supra* note 2, at 11.

[49]Here, the label "extremist" is intended to evoke the pejorative connotations not necessarily attached to extreme concepts.

[50]*See, e.g.*, William A. Gamson, *The Success of the Unruly*, *in* SOCIAL MOVEMENTS 357 (Doug McAdam and David A. Snow eds., 1997); Doug McAdam, *Tactical Innovation and the Pace of Insurgency*, *in* SOCIAL MOVEMENTS 340 (Doug McAdam and David A. Snow eds., 1997); Peter D. Moss, *Conflict and Containment in Television News: A Case Study*, *in* FRAMING FRICTION 161 (Mary S. Mander ed., 1999).

[51]CHAFEE, *supra* note 1, at 561.

Thomas Jefferson and many of his contemporaries apparently understood and embraced the value of radicalism in a pluralistic, democratic society.[52] The Madisonian view of government required more than the mere existence and availability of radical dissent in the marketplace of ideas. To assure the active pursuit of truth and a truly representative government, James Madison suggested, required a significant number of citizens to be exposed to dissident views.[53] Madison believed limited public exposure to radical dissent would "simultaneously violate the commitments to political equality and political deliberation"[54] upon which American government was founded. A modern interpretation of this view suggests that all citizens have both a right and an obligation to hear and consider even the most extreme political ideas.[55]

Jefferson at times held an even more radical position; he occasionally advocated the absolute freedom to engage in extreme and intemperate discussion of political issues, even when such discussion might lead to the dissolution of the existing government.[56] More than once Jefferson suggested that a country founded upon the liberty of its people must embrace not only the expression of extreme ideas but also the violent, armed resistance to government that may inevitably result from such ideas.[57] It was Jefferson who wrote: "I hold a little rebellion now and then is a good thing, and as necessary in the political world as storms in the physical."[58]

The Supreme Court has not endorsed this perspective. Thus, it was in a 1972 dissent that Justice Douglas wrote: "Advocacy of basic fundamental changes in government, which might popularly be described as 'overthrow,' is within the protection of the First Amendment even when [that amendment] is restrictively construed."[59]

---

[52] *Id.* at 19.

[53] SUNSTEIN, *supra* note 19, at xvi–xvii.

[54] *Id.* at 22.

[55] *Id. See also* Red Lion Broad. v. FCC, 395 U.S. 367 (1969); Jerome Barron, *Access to the Press—A New First Amendment Right*, 80 HARV. L. REV. 641 (1967).

[56] *See* CHAFEE, *supra* note 1, at 191; LEVY, *supra* note 17, at 301; SIEBERT, *supra* note 2, at 11.

[57] *See, e.g.*, Thomas Jefferson, *Letter to W. S. Smith, Nov. 13, 1787, quoted in* CHAFEE, *supra* note 1, at 191 ("What country can preserve its liberties if their rulers are not warned from time to time that their people preserve the spirit of resistance? Let them take arms.").

[58] WRITINGS OF JEFFERSON, *cited in* CHAFEE, *supra* note 1, at 191.

[59] Cole v. Richardson, 405 U.S. 676, 688 (1972) (Douglas, J., dissenting). *See also*, Parker v. Levy, 417 U.S. 733, 759 (1974) ("Disrespectful and contemptuous speech, even advocacy of violent change, is tolerable in the civilian community, for it does not directly affect the capacity of the Government to discharge its responsibilities unless it both is directed to inciting imminent lawless action and is likely to produce

DIVERGENT VOICES IN THE SCHOOLS

It is difficult to find a majority opinion for the Supreme Court that sweepingly endorses radical dissent.[60] The Court, however, at times has come close to expressing the Madisonian view of divergent ideas when reviewing government-imposed speech requirements in public schools. In dozens of rulings since the early 1900s, the Court has grappled with the limits of government power over speech and association in public schools and universities.[61] As early as its landmark 1943 decision in *West Virginia State Board of Education v. Barnette,* the Court proclaimed the unique importance of certain First Amendment values in public schools.[62] In the *Barnette* ruling that found a mandatory pledge and salute in the public schools unconstitutional, Justice Robert H. Jackson declared for the Court:

> We can have intellectual individualism and the rich cultural diversities that we owe to exceptional minds only at the price of occasional eccentricity and abnormal attitudes. When they are so harmless to others or to the State as those we deal with here, the price is not too great. *But freedom to differ is not limited to things that do not matter much. That would be a mere shadow of freedom. The test of its substance is the right*

---

such action."); Eisenstadt v. Baird, 405 U.S. 438, 459 (1972) (Douglas, J., concurring) ("The First Amendment protects the opportunity to persuade to action whether that action be unwise or immoral, or whether the speech incites to action."); Edwards v. South Carolina, 372 U.S. 229, 237 (1972) (The Constitution "does not permit a state to make criminal the peaceful expression of unpopular views."); Brandenburg v. Ohio, 395 U.S. 444, 447 (1969); Noto v. United States, 367 U.S. 290, 297–298 (1960) ("abstract teaching" of overthrow is protected activity."); Yates v. United States, 354 U.S. 298, 344 (1956) (Black, J., concurring in part, dissenting in part) ("The First Amendment ... leaves the way wide open for people to favor, discuss, advocate, or incite causes and doctrines however obnoxious and antagonistic such views may be to the rest of us."); Terminiello v. Chicago, 337 U.S. 1, 30, 32 (1949) (Jackson, J., dissenting).

[60]*See, e.g.,* Califano v. Jobst, 434 U.S. 47, 54 (1977) (welfare review of marital status does not constitute effort by which "government seeks to foist orthodoxy on the unwilling").

[61]*See, e.g.,* Wallace v. Jaffree, 472 U.S. 38 (1985); Perry Ed. Ass'n v. Perry Local Educators' Ass'n, 460 U.S. 37 (1983); Bd. of Ed. v. Pico, 457 U.S. 853 (1982); Widmar v. Vincent, 454 U.S. 263 (1981); Papish v. Bd. of Curators of Univ. of Missouri, 410 U.S. 667 (1973); Healy v. James, 408 U.S. 169 (1972); Tinker v. Des Moines Indep. Cmty Sch. Dist., 393 U.S. 503 (1969); Keyishian v. Bd. of Regents, 385 U.S. 589 (1967); Shelton v. Tucker, 364 U.S. 479 (1948); West Virginia State Bd. of Ed. v. Barnette, 319 U.S. 624 (1943); Minersville Sch. Dist. v. Gobitis, 310 U.S. 586 (1940); Hamilton v. Regents of Univ. of California, 293 U.S. 245 (1934); Pierce v. Society of Sisters, 268 U.S. 510 (1925); Meyer v. Nebraska, 262 U.S. 390 (1923); Waugh v. Mississippi, 237 U.S. 589 (1915).

[62]319 U.S. 624, 642 (1943).

> *to differ as to things that touch the heart of the existing order.* ... If there is any fixed star in our constitutional constellation, it is that no official, high or petty, can prescribe what shall be orthodox in politics, nationalism, religion, or other matters of opinion or force citizens to confess by word or act their faith therein. If there are any circumstances which permit an exception, they do not now occur to us.[63]

In the nearly sixty years since *Barnette*, the Court repeatedly has reasoned that government-imposed orthodoxy in the schools is a problem of unique concern.[64] Yet the heightened solicitude for unorthodox speech in public schools has not led the Court consistently to strike down speech requirements or prohibitions imposed on public teachers or students.[65] In 1952, Justice Douglas wrote in dissent to the Court's *Adler v. Board of Education* decision to allow schools to regulate teachers' speech to avoid "pollution"[66] of the public schools. He chastised the Court for forgetting that "[t]he Framers knew the danger of dogmatism; they also knew the strength that comes when the mind is free, when ideas may be pursued wherever they lead."[67]

In 1957, when the Court found a loyalty oath requirement for university faculty unconstitutional on First Amendment grounds, a concurrence by Justice Felix Frankfurter came close to broad advocacy of dissent.[68] In *Sweezy v. New Hampshire*, Justice Frankfurter reasoned that government-induced dogma is inimical to the First Amendment. He wrote: "[T]he spirit of free inquiry ... implies the right to examine, question, modify or reject traditional ideas and beliefs. Dogma and hypothesis are incompatible, and the concept of an immutable doctrine is repugnant to the spirit of a university."[69] But Justice Frankfurter limited his concern to the academic environment and failed to repudiate government-enforced dogma as repugnant to the universal inquiry and debate upon which democracy and the pursuit of truth rest.

---

[63]*Id.* at 641 (emphasis added).

[64]*See* Santa Fe Ind. Sch. Dist. v. Doe, 530 U.S. 290 (2000); Rosenberger v. Rector & Visitors of Univ. of Va., 515 U.S. 819 (1995); Zobrest v. Catalina Foothills Sch. Dist., 509 U.S. 1 (1993); Lee v. Weisman, 505 U.S. 577 (1992); Hazelwood Sch. Dist. v. Kuhlmeier, 484 U.S. 260 (1988); Sch. Dist. v. Ball, 473 U.S. 373 (1985); Sch. Dist. v. Schempp, 374 U.S. 203 (1963).

[65]*See, e.g.*, Adler v. Bd. of Educ., 342 U.S. 485 (1952) (upholding limits on public teachers' freedom to advocate violent overthrow).

[66]*Id.* at 493.

[67]*Id.* at 511 (Douglas, J., dissenting).

[68]Sweezy v. New Hampshire, 354 U.S. 234 (1957).

[69]*Id.* at 262 (Frankfurter, J., concurring).

In 1967, Justice William J. Brennan, writing for the Court, vehemently rejected the right of government to impose loyalty oaths on university faculty to weed out "subversives" and Communists.[70] While protecting teachers from government orthodoxy, the language of Justice Brennan's opinion in *Keyishian v. Board of Regents* again suggests that those inside schools enjoy greater protection of free speech than those outside. He wrote:

> Our Nation is deeply committed to safeguarding academic freedom, which is of transcendent value to all of us and not merely to the teachers concerned. That freedom is therefore a special concern of the First Amendment, which does not tolerate laws that cast a pall of orthodoxy over the classroom. 'The vigilant protection of constitutional freedoms is nowhere more vital than in the community of American schools.' The classroom is peculiarly the 'marketplace of ideas.' The Nation's future depends upon leaders trained through wide exposure to that robust exchange of ideas which discovers truth 'out of a multitude of tongues, [rather] than through any kind of authoritative selection.'[71]

In fact, since *Keyishian* the Court has decreasingly perceived government control of speech in the unique free speech sanctuary of the schools as unconstitutional government-imposed orthodoxy.[72] A quartet of cases that forms the foundation of the Supreme Court's modern academic speech jurisprudence demonstrates the Court's shifting reasoning and declining protection of dissenting or unpopular ideas in schools.

First, in *Tinker v. Des Moines Independent Community School District*, the Court limited school authority to control student dissent.[73] In *Tinker*, the Court underscored the constitutional strictures on government suppression of student speech:

> In our system, state-operated schools may not be enclaves of totalitarianism. School officials do not possess absolute authority over their students. Students in school as well as out of school are "persons" under our Constitution. They are possessed of fundamental rights, which the State must respect, just as they themselves must respect their obligations to the State.[74]

---

[70]Keyishian v. Bd. of Regents, 385 U.S. 589, 592 (1967).

[71]*Id.* at 603 (citations omitted).

[72]*But see* Bd. of Ed. v. Pico Ind. Sch. Dist., 457 U.S. 853 (1982); Tinker v. Des Moines Indep. Cmty Sch. Dist., 393 U.S. 503 (1969).

[73]393 U.S. 503, 509 (1969).

[74]*Id.* at 511.

The Court held in *Tinker* that high school officials could punish student political protest in school only when the expression materially or substantially disrupted educational activities.

In 1982, in *Board of Education v. Pico,*[75] the Court continued the line of *Tinker* and *Barnette* and demonstrated its willingness to view school action as unconstitutional suppression and imposition of orthodoxy. In *Pico* the Court rejected the power of public school officials to intentionally limit student exposure to diverse ideas by removing books from the school library. Wrote Justice Brennan for the Court:

> If petitioners *intended* by their removal decision to deny respondents access to ideas with which petitioners disagreed, and if this intent was the decisive factor in petitioners' decision, then petitioners have exercised their discretion in violation of the Constitution. To permit such intentions to control official actions would be to encourage the precise sort of officially prescribed orthodoxy unequivocally condemned in *Barnette.*[76]

The Court did not require clear evidence of pernicious government intent, however. Instead, the Court condemned the school action merely based on the fact that

> The evidence plainly does not foreclose the possibility that petitioners' decision to remove the books rested decisively upon disagreement with constitutionally protected ideas in those books, or upon a desire on petitioners' part to impose upon the students of the Island Trees High School and Junior High School a political orthodoxy to which petitioners and their constituents adhered.[77]

Four years later, in *Bethel School District v. Fraser,*[78] however, the Court affirmed the power of school officials to sanction a lewd student campaign speech that did not disrupt school activities but that *might* have been perceived to bear the school's endorsement or to reflect upon the educational mission of the school. Rather than view the school's action as an infringement of the student's fundamental rights, the Court emphasized the school's vital role to inculcate morals and values.[79] Accordingly, the Court reasoned, "The undoubted

[75]475 U.S. 853 (1982).
[76]*Id.* at 871 (emphasis in original).
[77]*Id.* at 875.
[78]478 U.S. 675 (1986).
[79]*Id.* at 681.

freedom to advocate unpopular and controversial views in schools and classrooms must be balanced against the society's countervailing interest in teaching students the boundaries of socially appropriate behavior."[80]

Then, in 1988, the Court, in *Hazelwood School District v. Kuhlmeier*, continued its *Fraser* reasoning when it effectively expanded the power of school officials to limit even non-lewd and non-disruptive student speech in school-sponsored public forums if school officials believed the expression did not conform to school values.[81] In an opinion seemingly devoid of solicitude for the marketplace of ideas so vital to education, the Court wrote:

> Educators are entitled to exercise greater control over ... student expression to ensure that participants learn whatever lessons the activity is designed to teach, that readers or listeners are not exposed to material that may be inappropriate for their level of maturity, and that the views of the individual speaker are not erroneously attributed to the school.[82]

In a 1995 decision requiring a public university to distribute student fees to support religious groups, the Supreme Court viewed denial of funding as a form of viewpoint discrimination prohibited by the First Amendment.[83] The Court reasoned that "[r]eligion may be a vast area of inquiry, but it also provides, as it did here, a specific premise, a perspective, a standpoint from which a variety of subjects may be discussed and considered."[84] To systematically exclude this perspective, the Court said, demonstrated an unacceptable government antipathy toward religious ideas.[85]

Two rulings handed down five years later suggest the Court continued to struggle to determine when religious expression—a form of divergent expression—in the academic environment deserved government encouragement[86] and when it might constitutionally be limited or eliminated.[87] While some would argue that these cases properly should be considered only as establishment clause decisions, the Court itself advanced the speech interests in the contested

[80]*Id.*
[81]484 U.S. 260 (1988).
[82]*Id.* at 271.
[83]Rosenberger v. Rector of the Univ. of Virginia, 515 U.S. 819 (1995).
[84]*Id.* at 831.
[85]*Id.* at 829–831.
[86]Bd. of Regents of Univ. of Wisconsin Sys. v. Southworth, 529 U.S. 217 (2000).
[87]Sante Fe Ind. School Dist. v. Doe, 530 U.S. 290 (2000).

religious activities by narrowly defining establishment clause violations[88] and by holding that private, non-government religious expression is protected by the free speech clause.[89]

In *Board of Regents v. Southworth,* the Court seemed to adopt a Madisonian perspective when it held that a university not only *may* but *must* support all types of messages within the public forums it establishes.[90] The Court said university support of unpopular religious speech in a university-funded forum advanced the university's mission. "Its mission is well served if students have the means to engage in dynamic discussions of philosophical, religious, scientific, social, and political subjects in their extracurricular campus life outside the lecture hall,"[91] the Court said. In contrast, that same year in *Santa Fe Independent School District v. Doe*, the Court held that constitutionally mandated government neutrality required high school officials to prohibit non-sectarian "prayers" before school-sponsored football games.[92] In this decision, the Court empowered schools to ban religious messages that might be perceived as government speech.

Scholars historically have argued that the Court's determination of constitutionality in these academic speech cases turns on the maturity of the audience; government power may be used to protect immature school children from divergent perspectives, but college students benefit from the diverse insights gained through exposure to these same ideas.[93] The Court, however, blurred this line in 1990 when it said "secondary students are mature enough and are likely to understand that a school does not endorse or support student speech that it merely permits on a nondiscriminatory basis."[94] Then, in 2001, the Court applied university precedents to the elementary-school setting to find that elementary school students did not require government protection from

[88]*Bd. of Regents of Univ. of Wisconsin Sys.*, 529 U.S. at 233.

[89]*Santa Fe Indep. Sch. Dist.*, 530 U.S. at 302.

[90]529 U.S. 217, 235 (2000). *See also* Susan Dente Ross, *Silenced Students*, 79 JOURNALISM AND MASS COMM. Q. 172 (2002).

[91]*Id.* at 232.

[92]530 U.S. 290, 302 (2000).

[93]Heather K. Lloyd, *NOTE & COMMENT: Injustice in Our Schools: Students' Free Speech Rights Are Not Being Vigilantly Protected*, 21 N. ILL. U. L. REV. 265 (2001); Richard L. Roe, *Valuing Student Speech: The Work of the Schools as Conceptual Development*, 79 CALIF. L. REV. 1271 (1991); W. Stuart Stuller, *High School Academic Freedom: The Evolution of a Fish out of Water*, 77 NEB. L. REV. 301 (1998); Lowell V. Sturgill, Jr. & Nancy S. Oliver, *NOTE: Religious Expression in the Public School Forum: The High School Student's Right to Free Speech*, 72 GEO. L.J. 135 (1983); Garner K. Weng, *Type No Evil: The Proper Latitude of Public Educational Institutions in Restricting Expressions of Their Students on the Internet*, 20 HASTINGS COMM. & ENT. L.J. 751 (1998);

[94]Bd. of Ed. v. Mergens, 496 U.S. 226, 250 (1990).

religious messages in school after hours.[95] The key to these academic speech rulings is far from clear, and the Court's protection of dissent in public schools is far from certain.[96]

POLITICAL DISSENT IN TIMES OF WAR AND FEAR

The Supreme Court has said robust discussion is of paramount value in the realm of politics.[97] In expressing this concept of the First Amendment, historian Alexander Meiklejohn wrote, "The guarantee given by the First Amendment is not ... assured to all speaking. It is assured only to speech which bears, directly or indirectly, upon [that] which voters have to deal—only, therefore, to the considerations of matters of public interest."[98] While continuing debate surrounds the parameters of "public interest" and political speech,[99] most scholars accept the notion that the core value of the First Amendment is to advance open discussion about issues relating to government, its actors and its actions.

In 1937, a unanimous Court announced the principle in *DeJonge v. Oregon*.[100] The Court wrote:

> The greater the importance of safeguarding the community from incitements to the overthrow of our institutions by force and violence, the more imperative is the need to preserve inviolate the constitutional rights of free speech, free press and free assembly in order to maintain the opportunity for free political discussion, to the end that government may be responsive to the will of the people and that changes, if desired, may be obtained by peaceful means. Therein lies the security of the Republic, the very foundation of constitutional government.[101]

---

[95]Good News Club v. Milford Central Sch., 533 U.S. 98, 114 (2001).

[96]*See* Susan Dente Ross, *Silenced Students*, 79 JOURNALISM AND MASS COMM. Q. 172 (2002).

[97]*See, e.g.*, Buckley v. Valeo, 424 U.S. 1, 15 (1976) ("It can hardly be doubted that the constitutional guarantee has its fullest and most urgent application precisely to the conduct of campaigns for political office."); New York Times v. United States, 403 U.S. 713, 729 (1971) (Brennan, J., concurring); New York Times v. Sullivan, 376 U.S. 254, 269 (1964); ALEXANDER MEIKLEJOHN, POLITICAL FREEDOM 54–55 (1960); Robert H. Bork, *Neutral Principles and Some First Amendment Problems*, 47 IND. L. J. 1, 20 (1971). *But see* Shiffrin, *supra* note 40, at 49.

[98]ALEXANDER MEIKLEJOHN, FREE SPEECH AND ITS RELATION TO SELF-GOVERNMENT 94 (1948).

[99]*See, e.g.*, Gentile v. State Bar of Nevada, 501 U.S. 1030, 1034 (1991) (defining lawyers' extrajudicial speech as political speech).

[100]299 U.S. 353 (1937) (striking down a state statute making it a crime to participate in a meeting conducted by Communists).

[101]*Id.* at 365.

More than six decades of Court opinions suggest, however, that the Court has not consistently preserved inviolate the rights and liberties of minorities and political dissidents.

While a full review of the relevant case law is not possible here, highlights will indicate the Court's difficulty in broadly advancing the speech and associational rights of those belonging to unpopular political groups or espousing radical ideas. The Court's highly speech- and association-restrictive rulings in sedition, espionage and Smith Act cases at the turn of the century and surrounding World War II are well known.[102] In addition, in the 1940s the Supreme Court found no constitutional violation in the military evacuation and detention of Japanese Americans during World War II[103] or the deportation after the end of the war of Germans legally in this country.[104] In neither case did the Court require government to show actual or intended violence by the subjects of the government orders. Similarly, from the 1950s to the 1970s the Supreme Court responded to pervasive fears of Communism by upholding a vast and varied body of laws and government actions limiting the freedoms of those associated with Communist and Marxist ideas.[105]

Exceptions to these suppressive rulings include an academic expression case, *Weiman v. Updegraff*,[106] striking down a state loyalty oath requirement for college faculty justified by vague fears of a leftist threat and *Yates v. United States*,[107] which remanded a Smith Act conviction because the law was, in part, unconstitutionally vague and allowed prosecution for constitutionally protected advocacy of ideas. Writing in concurrence to the Court's 1952 ruling in *Wieman*, Justice Black explained:

[102]*See, e.g.*, Scales v. United States, 360 U.S. 924 (1959); Dennis v. United States, 341 U.S. 494 (1951); Whitney v. California, 274 U.S. 357 (1927); Schenck v. United States, 249 U.S. 47 (1919); Frohwerk v. United States, 249 U.S. 204 (1919); Debs v. United States, 249 U.S. 211 (1919); Abrams v. United States, 250 U.S. 616 (1919). *See also* LEVY, *supra* note 17; WILLIAM PRESTON, ALIENS AND DISSENTERS: FEDERAL SUPPRESSION OF RADICALS, 1903–1933 (1963); JEFFERY SMITH, WAR AND PRESS FREEDOM (1999).

[103]Korematsu v. United States, 323 U.S. 214 (1944).

[104]Ludecke v. Watkins, 335 U.S. 160 (1948).

[105]*See, e.g.*, Kleindienst v. Mandel, 408 U.S. 753, 762 (1972); Scales v United States, 367 U.S. 203, 210 (1961); Carlson v Landon, 342 U.S. 524, 555 (1952); Dennis v. United States, 341 U.S. 494 (1951); Amer. Communications Ass'n v. Douds, 339 U.S. 382, 389 (1950). *But see* Wieman v. Updegraff, 344 U.S. 183, 192 (1952); Joint Anti-Fascist Refugee Committee v. McGrath, 341 US 123, 143 (1951).

[106]344 U.S. 183 (1952).

[107]Yates v. United States, 354 U.S. 298 (1957).

> It seems self-evident that all speech criticizing government rulers and challenging current beliefs may be dangerous to the status quo. With full knowledge of this danger the Framers rested our First Amendment on the premise that the slightest suppression of thought, speech, press, or public assembly is still more dangerous. This means that individuals are guaranteed an undiluted and unequivocal right to express themselves on questions of current public interest. It means that Americans discuss such questions as of right and not on sufferance of legislatures, courts or any other governmental agencies. It means that courts are without power to appraise and penalize utterances upon their notion that these utterances are dangerous. In my view this uncompromising interpretation of the Bill of Rights is the one that must prevail if its freedoms are to be saved. Tyrannical totalitarian governments cannot safely allow their people to speak with complete freedom. I believe with the Framers that our free Government can.[108]

Five years later, in *Yates*, Justice Black again argued in a separate opinion:

> [G]overnmental suppression of causes and beliefs seems to me to be the very antithesis of what our Constitution stands for. ... Unless there is complete freedom for expression of all ideas, whether we like them or not, concerning the way government should be run and who shall run it, I doubt if any views in the long run can be secured against the censor. The First Amendment provides the only kind of security system that can preserve a free government—one that leaves the way wide open for people to favor, discuss, advocate, or incite causes and doctrines however obnoxious and antagonistic such views may be to the rest of us.[109]

It would, perhaps, be unfair to say the Court honors this philosophy more in the breach than otherwise. However, even in cases dealing directly with political participation and advocacy, rousing statements of sweeping protection for antagonistic voices are often relegated to dissenting opinions.[110] Thus, in 1948 Justice Black dis-

[108]344 U.S. at 194 (Black, J., concurring).

[109]354 US at 344 (Black, J., dissenting in part).

[110]*See, e.g.,* Kleindienst v. Mandel, 408 U.S. 753, 773 (1972) (Douglas, J., dissenting); Scales v. United States, 367 U.S. 203, 262 (1961) (Black, J., dissenting); Communist Party of the United States v. Subversive Activities Control Bd., 367 U.S. 1, 137 (1961) (Black, J., dissenting); Carlson v. Landon, 342 U.S. 524, 555 (1952) (Black, J., dissenting); Amer. Communications Ass'n v. Douds, 339 U.S. 382, 449 (1950) (Black, J., dissenting); Ludecke v. Watkins, 335 U.S. 160, 184 (1948) (Douglas, J., dissenting); Korematsu v. United States, 323 US 214, 243 (1944) (Jackson, J., dissenting).

sented in *Ludecke v. Watkins* and reasoned that the deportation of Germans should be unconstitutional because "the First Amendment represents this nation's belief that the spread of political ideas must not be suppressed."[111] In another dissent, to a 1950 Court decision allowing government to demand non-Communist-affiliation oaths from union officials, Justice Black wrote:

> [N]ot the least of the virtues of the First Amendment is its protection of each member of the smallest and most unorthodox minority. Centuries of experience testify that laws aimed at one political or religious group, however rational these laws may be in their beginnings, generate hatreds and prejudices which rapidly spread beyond control. Too often it is fear which inspires such passions, and nothing is more reckless or contagious. In the resulting hysteria, popular indignation tars with the same brush all those who have ever been associated with any member of the group under attack or who hold a view which, though supported by revered Americans as essential to democracy, has been adopted by that group for its own purposes.[112]

Justice Black continued his stirring dissents, arguing against a 1952 Court decision permitting indefinite detention of suspected Communist aliens.[113] He argued for an absolute and unequivocal right of citizens to "believe in any governmental system, discuss all governmental affairs, and argue for desired changes in the existing order."[114] This unabridgeable right, Justice Black wrote, recognized the strength of the nation to withstand criticism and the fact that "we must have freedom of speech, press and religion for all or we may eventually have it for none."[115]

Nearly a decade later, Justice Black dissented in a case in which the Court upheld the authority of government to require registration of the Communist Party and its members.[116] Black reiterated his position "that the freedoms of speech, press, petition and assembly guaranteed by the First Amendment must be accorded to the ideas we hate

[111] 335 U.S. at 182 (Black, J., dissenting).

[112] Amer. Communications Ass'n v. Douds, 339 U.S. 382, 448–449 (1950) (Black, J., dissenting) (affirming national rule requiring union organizers to swear they have no Communist affiliations).

[113] Carlson v Landon, 342 U.S. 524, 555 (1952) (Black, J., dissenting) (allowing detention of alien Communist Party members pending final determination of their deportability).

[114] *Id.* (Black, J., dissenting).

[115] *Id.* (Black, J., dissenting).

[116] Communist Party of the United States v. Subversive Activities Control Bd., 367 U.S. 1, 96 (1961) (Black, J., dissenting).

or sooner or later they will be denied to the ideas we cherish."[117] He justified his stance by asserting the educational and corrective values of dissent and, he said, "Talk about the desirability of revolution has a long and honorable history."[118] Justice Black also argued that

> [A]ll the arguments and urgings the Communists and their sympathizers can use in trying to convert Americans to an ideology wholly foreign to our habits and our instincts are far less dangerous to the security of this Nation than laws which embark us upon a policy of repression by the outlawry of minority parties because they advocate radical changes in the structure of Government. This widespread program for punishing ideas on the ground that they might impair the internal security of the Nation not only sadly fails to protect that security but also diverts our energies and thoughts from the many far more important problems that face us as a Nation in this troubled world.[119]

In 1961, Justice Douglas joined the cry for liberty of expression in his dissent to the Court's decision to affirm a Smith Act conviction for Communist party membership in *Scales v. United States*.[120] He sharply criticized the Court's decision as a "break" with First Amendment tradition. The Court, he wrote, "make[s] serious Mark Twain's light-hearted comment that 'It is by the goodness of God that in our country we have those three unspeakably precious things: freedom of speech, freedom of conscience, and the prudence never to practice either of them.'"[121]

More than a decade later, Justice Douglas again dissented, this time to the exclusion of a foreign Marxist economist invited to speak at several prestigious U.S. academic institutions.[122] He directly challenged the government's asserted interest in protecting national security and preventing "the infiltration of saboteurs."[123] He found no merit to the national security claim and said the attorney general instead was simply "stand[ing] astride our international terminals" as a national censor engaged in "thought control" and barring entry to individuals who could educate U.S. citizens by exposing them to new ideas.[124] Douglas asserted that limiting entry only to individuals

[117] *Id.* at 137 (Black, J., dissenting).
[118] *Id.* at 147 (Black, J., dissenting).
[119] *Id.* at 168 (Black, J., dissenting).
[120] 367 U.S. 203 (1961).
[121] *Id.* at 262 (Douglas, J., dissenting).
[122] Kleindienst v. Mandel, 408 U.S. 753, 773 (1972) (Douglas, J., dissenting).
[123] *Id.* at 772 (Douglas, J., dissenting).
[124] *Id.* (Douglas, J., dissenting).

whose ideas the attorney general approved advanced no valid government purpose.

Justice Thurgood Marshall expressed broad liberty concerns in his 1974 dissent to a Court opinion dismissing as premature and hypothetical an American Civil Liberties Union freedom of association challenge to a banking disclosure law.[125] The Court held that a federal law mandating disclosure of certain financial transactions to aid criminal investigations did not intrude unnecessarily on ACLU members' privacy and associational rights. Justice Marshall premised his resounding dissent largely upon the fragility of First Amendment freedoms and the tendency for their exercise to be easily deterred. He admonished the Court that it was properly the responsibility of government to show the compelling need for First Amendment-intrusive regulations, an obligation he said the government had failed entirely to meet. Facilitating law enforcement, he wrote,

> cannot justify the Government's running roughshod over the First Amendment rights of the hundreds of lawful yet controversial organizations like the ACLU. Congress may well have been correct in concluding that law enforcement would be facilitated by the dragnet requirements of this Act. Those who wrote our Constitution, however, recognized more important values.[126]

Although similar decisions appear throughout the 1970s, 1980s and 1990s, even a lone justice asserting expansive protection for dissent is difficult to find.[127] For example, Justice Black wrote a 1971 majority opinion overturning an injunction against a state criminal syndicalism prosecution and arguing that the chilling effect of the state's statute and prosecution is insufficiently severe to warrant injunctive relief.[128] By the late 1990s, only one[129] out of a group of cases

[125]California Bankers Ass'n. v. Schultz, 416 U.S. 21, 93 (1974) (Marshall, J., dissenting).

[126]*Id.* at 99 (Marshall, J., dissenting).

[127]*See, e.g.,* Reno v. Amer. Arab Anti-Discrimination Comm., 525 U.S. 471 (1999) (rejecting selective enforcement claim as grounds for court intervention in INS deportation proceeding); Chicago v. Morales, 527 U.S. 41 (1999) (plurality ruling finding ban on public loitering by two or more suspected gang members violates personal liberty and is unconstitutionally vague); Boos v. Barry, 485 U.S. 312 (1988) (finding ban on demonstrations outside foreign consulates unconstitutional); Younger v. Harris, 401 U.S. 37 (1971).

[128]Younger v. Harris, 401 U.S. 37 (1971). *See also* Samuels v. Mackell, 401 U.S. 66 (1971)

[129]Reno v. Amer. Arab Anti-Discrimination Comm., 525 U.S. 471 (1999), *vacat'g and remand'g*, 119 F.3d 1367 (9th Cir. 1997).

claiming government infringement of the speech and association rights of dissident aliens accused of affiliation with terrorist organizations[130] was accepted for review by the Supreme Court.

In *Reno v. American Arab Anti-Discrimination Committee*, the Court held that eight aliens facing deportation under the Anti-Terrorism and Effective Death Penalty Act of 1996[131] had failed to demonstrate that Immigration and Naturalization Service conduct was "flagrantly improper."[132] Absent such a showing, the Court said, any claim that selective INS enforcement of the law disproportionately chilled disfavored speech was insufficient to warrant judicial intervention when the statute itself strictly limited the role of federal courts in pending INS deportation proceedings.

In a concurring opinion, Justice John Paul Stevens offered small solace to those fearing sweeping abridgement of fundamental freedoms premised upon tenuous and speculative claims of terrorist activity. "Of course," he wrote, "Congress could not authorize punishment of innocent persons because they happen to be members of an organization that engaged in terrorism."[133] The ruling itself, however, and others like it do not make clear why we should hold this faith. Indeed, potentially innocent association with organizations labeled terrorist by government fiat does now provide the basis for detention of more than a thousand and deportation for some.[134]

---

[130]*See, e.g.,* Ashcroft v. Humanitarian Law Project, 532 U.S. 904 (2001) (cert. denied); Humanitarian Law Project v. Reno, 205 F.3d 1130 (9th Cir. 2001), *cert. denied*, 532 U.S. 904 (2001); People's Mojahedin Org. of Iran v. United States, 182 F.3d 17 (D.C.Cir. 2000), *cert. denied*, 529 U.S. 1104 (2000); Reno v. Amer. Arab Anti-Discrimination Comm., 526 U.S. 1081 (1999) (reh'g denied). *See also* Susan Dente Ross, *In the Shadow of Terror: The Illusive First Amendment Rights of Aliens*, 6 COMM. LAW AND POL'Y 75 (2001).

[131]Antiterrorism and Effective Death Penalty Act, Pub. Law 104–132, 104 Cong. 2d (1996).

[132]525 U.S. 471, 498 (1999).

[133]*Id.* at 501 (Stevens, J., concurring).

[134]*See* Susan Dente Ross, *In the Shadow of Terror: The Illusive First Amendment Rights of Aliens*, 6 COMM. LAW AND POL'Y 75 (2001); Tom Brune, *They Can't See Eye-To-Eye; Leahy, Ashcroft Embattled Over Civil Rights Vs. Security*, NEWSDAY, Nov. 13, 2001, at A22; Tom Brune, *U.S. To Question Immigrants; Terror Probe Seeks 5,000 Who Fit Profile*, NEWSDAY, Nov. 14, 2001, at A62; *Cover Editorial: What Price Security?; In Search For Safety, U.S. Sacrifices Too Many Rights, 1,147 People Have Been Snared In Ashcroft's Terror Probe*, NEWSDAY, Nov. 25, 2001, at B02; Mark Helm, *Ashcroft Defends Anti-Terror Campaign; Attorney General Refuses To Back Down On Secrecy, Rounding Up Terrorists And Tribunals*, THE (ALBANY, N.Y.) TIMES UNION, Dec. 7, 2001, at A10; Mark Helm, *Ashcroft Calls For Tougher Terror Bills*, PITTSBURGH POST-GAZETTE, Oct. 5, 2001, at A10; Sonya Ross, *Police Get New Tools To Fight Terror; Wiretapping, Arrests Easier*, THE (BERGEN COUNTY, NJ) RECORD, Oct. 27, 2001, at A01.

A MODEST PROPOSAL TO INCREASE PROTECTION OF DISSENT

As the above review indicates, the Supreme Court's protection of dissent is uncertain and highly contextual, even when that speech involves political debate or occurs within the sanctuary of the schools. The Court's support for broad freedom of expression in the classroom is less than robust. The Court also has shaped the First Amendment to permit protection against diffuse or undemonstrated government fears rather than to advance the ideas of unpopular speakers. Too often the Court's balancing of interests pits a lone individual or a dissident group against perceived popular opinion and majoritarian interests. The thumb of political correctness weights the scales of justice against divergence, discord and dissent. The cost of the Court's less than zealous advocacy of free speech extends far beyond the lives of the individuals jailed, punished or deported. The harm reaches beyond the justice system to erode the fabric of our nation. The cost of suppression is a society in which difference is dangerous; neighbor turns against neighbor, destroying the societal cohesion government purports to advance.[135] The Court's adoption of a more speech-protective doctrine would promote the broad interests of democracy.[136]

The Court has applied the components of the test proposed here in various First Amendment contexts;[137] this approach simply brings aspects of various tests together to provide a strategy that reflects the fundamental constitutional presumption that government action, not freedom of speech and association, must be justified. Before explaining the test, however, it is important to recognize that the speech involved in all of the previously reviewed case law may be defined as political, in the sense that it comprises discussion of issues of public interest, self-governance and policy. The school expression cases hold special implications for the education and training of an

---

[135] *See* JOAN W. BLOS, OLD HENRY (1987) ("Maybe, some other time, we'd get along/ not thinking that somebody *has* to be wrong./ And we don't have to make such a terrible fuss/ because everyone isn't exactly like us."); CHAFEE, *supra* note 1, at 563, 564.

[136] *See, e.g.*, S.E. Wilborn Malloy & R.J. Krotoszynski, Jr., *Recalibrating the Cost of Harm Advocacy: Getting Beyond Brandenburg*, 41 WM. AND MARY L. REV. 1159 (2000) (proposing a test to permit punishment of harm advocacy).

[137] The concept for this analytical approach was suggested by the work of Malloy & Krotoszynski, Jr., *id.*, who adopt a related strategy to encourage punishment of what they call "harm advocacy."

informed polity, while the dissent and association cases go right to the heart of citizen debate and participation.

The proposed test weaves together several different threads of law. First, when government directly infringes upon core political speech, the Supreme Court has tended to review the government action under strict scrutiny.[138] When applying strict scrutiny, the Court assumes government action is unconstitutional unless the government can show with clear and convincing evidence that its action is the least speech-restrictive means of advancing a compelling government interest. Thus, the burden of proof to support the government action falls to the government, not the targeted speaker. The Court also has held that government may not impose orthodoxy or suppress ideas it disfavors.[139] However, the Court has permitted government regulation of speech that presents an imminent, demonstrable and significant danger to society[140] and speech that lacks any serious value.[141] Moreover, speakers who knowingly and intentionally cause harm to others or to compelling government interests may be subject to punishment.[142]

When these doctrines are combined to develop a test that protects dissent, it becomes clear that government action against dissidents would be permitted only when government shows convincingly that:

1. the purposes[143] and effects of the government action advance a compelling government interest unrelated to imposed orthodoxy or suppression of speech or association,
2. the need to constrain speech or association is real, substantial and imminent,[144]
3. the constrictions on speech and association are the least intrusive possible,

[138]*See, e.g.,* Nixon v. Shrink Missouri Gov't, 528 U.S. 377, 381 (1999); Buckley v. Am. Const. Law Found., 525 U.S. 182, 206 (1999) (O'Connor, J., concurring); Arkansas Educ. TV Consortium v. Forbes, 523 U.S. 666, 677 (1998); Burson v. Freeman, 504 U.S. 191, 197 (1991); Illinois St. Bd. of Elections v. Socialist Workers Party, 440 U.S. 173, 188 (1979) (Blackmun, J., concurring).

[139]*See* Ward v. Rock Against Racism, 491 U.S. 781, 791 (1991); Texas v. Johnson, 491 U.S. 397, 414 (1989); Bd. of Ed. v. Pico, 457 U.S. 853, 872 (1982); United States v. O'Brien, 391 U.S. 367, 375 (1968).

[140]*See* Brandenburg v. Ohio, 395 U.S. 444 (1969).

[141]*See* Miller v. California, 413 U.S. 15 (1973).

[142]*See* New York Times v. United States, 403 U.S. 713, 721 (Douglas, J., concurring), 737, 740 (White, J., concurring); New York Times v. Sullivan, 376 U.S. 254, 262, 284 (1964) (establishing the standard for restricting exemplary libel damages).

[143]*See* Bd. of Ed. v. Pico, 457 U.S. 853, 872 (1982).

[144]*See* California Bankers Ass'n. v. Schultz, 416 U.S. 21, 69 (1974).

4. the constrained speech or association, taken in context, lacks any serious value, and
5. the speaker knowingly engaged in the association or expression with intent to endanger the government's compelling interest.

APPLICATION OF THE TEST

In cases involving political dissent, the government regularly argues that its actions are necessary to advance the nation's compelling interest in security.[145] Clearly, the Court has said in *dicta*, protecting national security is a compelling interest.[146] However, as demonstrated in *New York Times v. United States*, the government action must respond to a real threat to national security, not some speculative, hypothetical or distant harm.[147] To pass this prong of the test, government must document the validity of its interest with convincing evidence. In addition, the government must show that the facially constitutional purpose of the government action does not hide any invidious, censorial objective.[148] In cases where a challenge to government action is based on claims of selective application, government also must demonstrate that the law, as applied, does not disproportionately harm disfavored speakers or organizations.[149]

For government action to pass constitutional muster, then, it will be necessary, but not sufficient, to demonstrate the importance and credibility of the government's non-discriminatory purpose and effects. Then the test requires that the need for government action be of sufficient magnitude and immediacy to warrant intrusion upon fundamental liberties.[150] Thus, mere advocacy of revolutionary ideas would not suffice, nor would tenuous associations with purportedly terrorist organizations. Under the standard, government could not rest its action upon vague assertions of generalized fears or distant

---

[145]*See* New York Times v. United States, 403 U.S. 713, 718 (1971) (Black, J., concurring).

[146]*See* Near v. Minnesota, 283 U.S. 697, 716 (1931).

[147]*New York Times,* 403 U.S. at 719 (Black, J., concurring). *See also* Turner Broad. Sys. v. FCC, 520 U.S. 180, 252 (1996) (O'Connor, J., concurring).

[148]*See* Bd. of Ed. v. Pico, 457 U.S. 853, 871–72 (1982).

[149]*See, e.g.,* Turner Broad. Sys. v. FCC, 520 U.S. 180, 222 (1996); Turner Broad. Sys. v. FCC, 512 U.S. 622, 647 (1994) (rejecting this position); *Turner Broad. Sys.,* 512 U.S. at 675–676 (O'Connor, J., dissenting); Leathers v. Medlock, 499 U.S. 439, 447 (1991); Buckley v. Valeo, 424 U.S. 1, 48–49 (1976).

[150]*See* Brandenburg v. Ohio, 395 U.S. 444, 447–48 (1969).

connections to violence.[151] Instead, government would be required to show with compelling evidence the substantial and immediate danger posed by the constrained individual's speech and/or membership at the time of government action.

Having met the first two hurdles, government would then be required to show that the detention, deportation, constriction of rights or confiscation of resources was essential to achieve the government's compelling interest and to avoid the substantial and imminent danger. It would not suffice to argue that national security is better advanced by jailing all individuals of a certain age and nationality, or that criminal investigations are facilitated by invading the freedoms and privacy of residents in this country. Rather, government action would be constitutional only if the government could demonstrate convincingly that it had considered and rejected as ineffective *all* other means of achieving the stated objective that would better protect personal liberties.[152]

Having assured the constitutional purpose and fit of the government action, the Court next would determine whether the government action harmed valuable or innocent speech and association. Thus, the final two prongs of the test would require the Supreme Court to examine whether the constrained speech had serious social or political value, or whether the speaker acted innocently and without knowledge of the dangers posed by the organizations to which she belonged.[153] If the speech were valuable to society, it would warrant First Amendment protection. If the speaker lacked *scienter*, he too would stand behind the First Amendment's shield.

Application of the proposed test would limit government action against political dissent to occasions when an individual knowingly and intentionally engaged in speech or associations that posed extreme danger to a compelling government interest without any counterbalancing social benefit. While this proposal falls short of Jefferson's position that even violent overthrow of government should be protected in a liberty-loving society, the proposed test would take a giant step toward protecting, and even encouraging, expression of non-conformist, anti-authoritarian or just plain unusual political views in this country.

---

[151]*See Turner Broad. Sys.*, 520 U.S. at 252 (O'Connor, J., dissenting); *New York Times,* 403 U.S. at 725 (Brennan, J., concurring).

[152]*See Turner Broad. Sys.*, 520 U.S. at 217 (1996).

[153]*See* Miller v. California, 413 U.S. 15, 18 (1973); Brandenburg v. Ohio, 395 U.S. 444, 453 (1969) (Douglas, J., concurring).

CONCLUSIONS

Some will argue that this proposal goes too far, that it ties the hands of a government rightly charged with protecting the safety of its citizens. Some will say I have failed to understand the true threat posed by conspiracies and terrorist cells. Some will even say I have fueled the efforts of those who would destroy this country and the freedom I claim to hold dear.

Perhaps they are right, but I think not. I think rather that we would do well to take seriously cartoonist Walt Kelly's light-hearted words: "We have met the enemy and he is us."[154] We are our own enemy whenever we are motivated not by faith in our own ideas and the power of democracy but by fear of fanaticism, Communism, Marxism, terrorism. As Franklin Delano Roosevelt said, "The only thing to fear is fear itself."[155] For in our fear, we willingly give up that which we otherwise would fight to defend.

As a nation, we have a choice. As Professor Chafee wrote nearly half a century ago:

> We must choose between freedom and fear—we cannot have both. If the citizens of the United States persist in being afraid, the real rulers of this country will be fanatics fired with a zeal to save grown men from objectionable ideas by putting them under the care of official nursemaids.[156]

The Supreme Court must not allow the government to act as nursemaid to its citizenry. The Court must reject paternalism and recognize that an informed, active polity thrives only amid radical dissent and controversial ideas. By encouraging wide-open public debate, the Supreme Court can protect our liberty *and* our safety; the Court need only use the tools it has at its disposal. If the Supreme Court will apply the rigorous scrutiny outlined above whenever government restricts fundamental liberties in times of national anxiety, ... if the Court will consistently advocate freedom in the face of fear, ... if the Court will embody the belief that dissonance and disagreement are the lifeblood of democracy, then, and only then, will we as a nation approach the participatory self-governance the framers intended. Then, and only then, will we be truly free to speak.

---

[154]Walt Kelly, *Pogo cartoon*, *in* BARTLETT'S FAMILIAR QUOTATIONS 398 (J. Bartlett & J. Kaplan eds., 16th ed., 1992).

[155]F.D. Roosevelt, *First Inaugural Address, March 4, 1933*, *in* BARTLETT'S FAMILIAR QUOTATIONS 648 (J. Bartlett & J. Kaplan eds., 16th ed., 1992).

[156]ZECHARIAH CHAFEE, JR., THE BLESSINGS OF LIBERTY 156 (1956).

7 COMM. L. & POL'Y 431–459 (2002)

ACADEMIC FREEDOM AND 9/11: HOW THE WAR ON TERRORISM THREATENS FREE SPEECH ON CAMPUS

R. KENTON BIRD*
ELIZABETH BARKER BRANDT**

College and university faculty members who have spoken out against U.S. foreign policy, particularly after the terrorist attacks on September 11, 2001, have been reprimanded, disciplined, harassed and, in one case, threatened with dismissal from a tenured position. This article explores the legal and philosophical roots of academic freedom, as well as the origins of tenure as a basis for protecting the rights of faculty members to investigate and speak freely on controversial issues. The authors examine several cases involving faculty members who criticized the U.S. government's military and foreign policy after 9/11, and the consequences they suffered. Finally, they assess the climate for academic freedom in the twenty-first century.

Colleges and universities in the United States have been the source of much of the critical thinking on public policy questions, especially during the twentieth century.[1] Because the university

---

*Assistant Professor, University of Idaho School of Communication.
**Professor, University of Idaho College of Law.

[1]Richard Hofstadter, a leading U.S. historian of the twentieth century, declared, "No one can or should underestimate the contributions of research to American life, nor the ideas which university scholars have given to the material and intellectual well-being of our society." Richard H. Hofstadter, *The Development of Higher Education in America*, *in* THE DEVELOPMENT AND SCOPE OF HIGHER EDUCATION IN THE UNITED STATES 66 (Richard H. Hofstadter & C. DeWitt Hardy eds., 1952). Similarly, Arthur M. Cohen wrote in his sweeping survey of American higher education history, "The Enlightenment dream was that debates on justice and equity would take place in a public arena, that an ever-evolving quest for truth would replace tradition.

has traditionally been somewhat insulated from the pressures of public and political life, it has provided the distance that is often necessary for reasoned reflection and critique. Not only have colleges and universities played a pivotal role in shaping national thinking on public issues, they have furnished a laboratory in which many students develop their own world views for the first time. A world view is shaped not only by traditional learning methods (reading, reflection and classroom discussion) but also through reacting to, critiquing and debating national and world events. Universities have been able to fulfill this function largely because academic freedom, at least in theory, protects the free exchange of ideas.[2] Colleges and universities in this country are neither instruments of the state nor subversive organizations that challenge state mandates. They usually operate at some distance from other aspects of American life and culture. Critics of higher education sometimes denigrate the "ivory tower" mentality of these institutions, yet it is this very insularity that enables scientific, political and artistic ideas to form, evolve and win acceptance without being unduly influenced by economic necessity and popular opinion.

The concept of academic freedom, as understood in most American universities, developed from a number of sources: European values of free thought and mind,[3] nineteenth century American

Research, experimentation and rational inquiry in the universities fit the dream." ARTHUR M. COHEN, THE SHAPING OF AMERICAN HIGHER EDUCATION: EMERGENCE AND GROWTH OF THE CONTEMPORARY SYSTEM 129 (1998).

[2]Arthur O. Lovejoy, one of the founders and early leaders of the American Association of University Professors, observed in the 1930 edition of the *Encyclopedia of Social Sciences*, that the ultimate social good of a university "'is rendered impossible if the work of the investigator is shackled by the requirement that his conclusions shall never seriously deviate from the generally accepted beliefs or from those accepted by the persons, private or official, through whom society provides the means for the maintenance of universities,'" *quoted in* William W. Van Alstyne, *Academic Freedom and the First Amendment in the Supreme Court of the United States: An Unhurried Historical Review*, 53 L. & CONTEMP. PROBS. 79, 87 (1990). C. DeWitt Hardy, in a companion essay to Richard Hofstadter's historical survey, *supra* note 1, noted, "The violence of the controversy around [the social scientist] is a measure of the social importance of what he is doing, the critical value of what he may discover. ... His research will bring tenseness into the academic community, a sharp, bracing air from the outside world." C. DeWitt Hardy, *The Scope of Higher Education in America, in* THE DEVELOPMENT AND SCOPE OF HIGHER EDUCATION IN THE UNITED STATES, *supra* note 1, at 203.

[3]*General Report of the Committee on Academic Freedom and Academic Tenure*, 1 AAUP BULL., Dec. 1915, at 17, *reprinted in Appendix A: General Report of the Committee on Academic Freedom and Academic Tenure* (1915), 53 L. & CONTEMP. PROBS. 393 (1990) [hereinafter 1915 Declaration]. The 1915 Declaration drew heavily on the German concept of *lehrfreiheit*—the "freedom to teach." *See* Walter A. Metzger, *The 1940 Statement of Principles on Academic Freedom and Tenure*, 53 L. &

values of individualism and libertarianism[4] and twentieth century norms of free speech.[5] Yet the prevailing ideal of academic freedom in today's colleges and universities is broader than any of its constituent parts. Its main power is not in its enforceability as law, but rather in the broad-based commitment by participants both inside and outside higher education to defend and perpetuate the ideal.[6] In fact, academic freedom is only enforced by courts in very limited situations.[7]

The terrorist attacks on the United States on September 11, 2001, have changed the ways in which many Americans think about freedom and security issues. The world reacted with shock and horror to the calamitous attacks on the World Trade Center and the Pentagon and the crash of a hijacked jet in Pennsylvania. After the initial emotional response, Americans sought to understand the conditions that led to the attack while government officials imposed security measures in an attempt to prevent it from happening again. President George W. Bush rhetorically declared a war on terrorism[8] and won support from Congress for military action against groups in Afghanistan linked to terrorist groups.[9]

CONTEMP. PROBS. 3, 14–15 (1990). William Van Alstyne, points to the Miltonian roots of academic freedom. Van Alstyne, *supra* note 2, at 86.

[4]Walter A. Metzger points out a number of philosophical traditions that underpin the 1915 Declaration, including Millsian market libertarianism. Metzger, *supra* note 3, at 13. *See also* Van Alstyne, *supra* note 2, at 86.

[5]The connection between late twentieth century free speech norms and current understandings of academic freedom is explored *infra* notes 31–75 and accompanying text.

[6]William Van Alstyne has referred to the notion of academic freedom embodied in the American Association of University Professor 1940 Statement of Principles as "soft law" because it is not often enforced by courts. Rather, the 1940 Statement is enforced primarily through the voluntary response of colleges and universities to AAUP investigations and censure. Van Alstyne, *supra* note 2, at 79–80.

[7]As we point out later, academic freedom may be enforced by courts to the extent that government interferes with free speech in the institutional context of universities. *See, e.g.* Sweezy v. New Hampshire, 354 U.S. 234, 250 (1957)(recognizing that free speech at universities is essential to their functioning), to the extent that public universities impermissibly infringe on the free speech of faculty members or students; and Healy v. James, 408 U.S. 169 (1972), discussed *infra* notes 81–83 and accompanying text. To the extent principles of academic freedom are incorporated in the terms of employment contracts, *see infra* notes 38–39 and accompanying text.

[8]Bush spoke to a joint session of Congress Sept. 20, 2001. *See* Doyle McManus, *After the Attack; The President; Bush Vows Firm 'Justice,' Lists Demands to Taliban*, L.A. TIMES, Sept. 21, 2001, at A1.

[9]Of particular concern to civil libertarians is the sweeping anti-terrorism law approved by Congress in an eighteen-hour period in October 2001. The law is known as the USA Patriot Act, Public L. No. 107–56, 115 Stat. 272 (2001). It includes provisions allowing the government to wiretap phones a terrorism suspect might use with a single warrant and promoting sharing of information among law enforcement and intelligence agencies. *See* Mark G. Young, *What Big Eyes and Ears You Have!: A*

As with past U.S. foreign policy crises, university professors and, to a lesser degree, students have raised questions about the causes and consequences of the events of 9/11.[10] Criticism of U.S. policy has been denounced as counterproductive and even seditious.[11] Attorney General John Ashcroft dismissed concerns about the potential loss of freedoms, saying the complaints "only aid terrorists, for they erode our national unity."[12] White House Press Secretary Ari Fleischer warned Americans to "watch what they say, watch what they do."[13] Senate Republican Leader Trent Lott accused his Democratic counterpart, Senator Tom Daschle, of undermining the president's authority as commander-in-chief by questioning the open-ended nature of the war in Afghanistan.[14] When questions arose about the government's failure to act on U.S. intelligence agencies' reports in the summer of 2001 about the possibility of terrorist attacks, Vice President Dick Cheney called the speculation "thoroughly irresponsible ... in a time of war."[15] Even pacifists, such as National Public Radio Weekend Edition host Scott Simon, concluded that there was "no sane alternative but to support the war."[16]

New Regime for Governmental Surveillance, 79 FORD. L. REV. 1017 (2001); Robin Toner and Neil A. Lewis, *A Nation Challenged; Congress; House Passes Terrorism Bill Much Like Senate's, But With 5-Year Limit,* N.Y. TIMES, Oct. 13, 2002, at B6.

[10]We will refer to the crashes at the World Trade Centers, the Pentagon and in rural Pennsylvania, collectively, as the events of 9/11. The American Dialect Society and Center for Applied Linguistics, among other groups, has documented the use of this term to refer to the disaster. *See* Erin McClam, *Nation Settles on Term "9/11" to Refer to Terrorist Attacks,* CHATTANOOGA TIMES/CHATTANOOGA FREE PRESS, Mar. 21, 2002, at A2.

[11]*See, e.g.,* Lewis H. Lapham, *American Jihad,* HARPER'S MAG., Jan. 2002, at 7 (explaining that experts critical of the war on terrorism do not want to appear on news programs because of fear they would appear seditious).

[12]Dan Eggan, *Ashcroft Defends Anti-Terrorism Steps; Civil Liberties Groups' Attacks "Only Aid Terrorists" Senate Panel Told,* WASH. POST, Dec. 7, 2001, at A40.

[13]Associated Press Online, *White House Reprimands Maher, available at* 2001 WL 28012582 (Sept. 26, 2001).

[14]Janet Hook, *Daschle Questions Future Success of U.S. War Effort,* L.A. TIMES, Mar. 1, 2002, at A1.

[15]Judy Keen, *White House Defends Its Actions On Hijack Warnings,* USA TODAY, May 17, 2002, at 1A.

[16]Scott Simon, Reflections on the Events of September 11, address at the Nineteenth Annual Ethics in Telecommunications Lecture, sponsored by the Office of Communication, Inc. of the United Church of Christ and the Telecommunications Research and Action Center, Sept. 25, 2001, *quoted in* Patricia A. Hart, The Simonized War in Afghanistan: A Quaker Calls for the Silencing of Peace Activists 1 (Apr. 20, 2002)(paper presented at the Pacific Northwest American Studies conference in Spokane, Wash.)(unpublished manuscript on file with the authors). *See also* Scott Simon, *Even Pacifists Must Support this War,* WALL ST. J., Oct. 11, 2001, at A22.

These comments have contributed to a climate in which freedom of speech in the United States is less secure today than it was before the events of 9/11. This chilly climate for speech extends not only to our general public policy discourse, but also to the intellectual discourse of our colleges and universities. Oral and written remarks critical of U.S. policy appear to be most at risk, although several situations involving restrictions on display of American flags or pro-government slogans also have been documented.[17] In only one of the higher education cases has a faculty member been threatened with dismissal.[18] But in others, the tone of the criticism suggests an intolerance for dissent that may discourage professors from speaking publicly about the war or its domestic consequences.[19] Given the idealistic nature of academic freedom, the chilly speech climate will most likely lead to self-censorship by faculty members unwilling to risk harassment, intimidation or informal retribution.[20]

To their credit, some university presidents have eloquently defended the right of their students and faculty members to speak and write contrarian and unpopular ideas.[21] However, the failure of other

---

[17]Many of these cases have been documented by Foundation for Individual Rights in Education and are published on its Web site, http://www.thefire.org (visited Mar. 29, 2002). The incidents involving the display of patriotic symbols detailed on the FIRE Web site arose at Central Michigan University, where students were asked to remove patriotic posters from their dormitory, and at the College of Holy Cross, where a department chair removed a U.S. flag displayed in the departmental office by a secretary. *See infra* note 102 and accompanying text.

[18]Sami Al-Arian, a professor of computer science at the University of South Florida, as of May 20, 2002, was on a paid leave of absence, awaiting the university president's decision to fire or reinstate him. See *infra* notes 105–116 and accompanying text.

[19]Several commentators expressed concern about the motives and methods of Americans for Victory Over Terrorism, a group led by former Education Secretary William Bennett. *USA Today* columnist Walter Shapiro suggested that Bennett and other AVOT founders "seem determined to create an anti-war movement in order to defeat it." *Anti-Anti-War Crowd Dreams Up a Disloyal Opposition,* USA TODAY, Mar. 13, 2002, at 5A. David Corn, a columnist for *The Nation,* wrote in March 2002, "Bennett and his Americans for Victory Over Terrorism lieutenants are trying to chill discourse when they say certain criticism of the war is out of bounds." David Corn, *The Loyal Opposition: Soundbite Patriots; Can Free Speech Undermine Freedom?* http://www.tompaine.com/feature.cfm/ID/5268 (posted Mar. 15, 2002; accessed May 19, 2002).

[20]Robert Jensen, who was criticized by the president of the University of Texas for his comments critical of U.S. policy after 9/11, writes, "At various times in my teaching career—more than ever since Sept. 11—I have been advised by faculty colleagues that I should avoid being 'too political' in the classroom." Robert Jensen, *September 11 and the Politics of University Teaching*, http://uts.cc.utexas.edu/~rjensen/freelance/attack19.htm (visited Mar. 29, 2002).

[21]The AAUP's Committee on Academic Freedom and Tenure quoted Shirley Strum Kenny, president of the State New York at Stony Brook, as saying, "It is in-

presidents to forcefully defend free speech on campus, to political leaders and to the public undermines academic freedom. Such a defense is critical to the ongoing integrity of the tradition. Recent public statements by university leaders distancing themselves and their institutions from faculty who are critical of U.S. policy are further evidence of a deep breakdown in the consensus that has supported academic freedom. The prevailing public mood also seems inclined to restrict statements by faculty members critical of official U.S. policy.[22] Although this reaction is consistent with the ways in which Americans attempted to suppress dissent during the twentieth century, especially during wars and times of perceived threats to national security, the threat to academic freedom is the most significant since the early period of the Cold War and the protests of the Vietnam War.

In this article, we argue that in times of national crisis, the public's support for the broad conceptual notion of academic freedom begins to erode—just as support for other freedoms wavers. This erosion is especially troubling because the continuing viability of academic freedom depends not on court enforcement, but rather on the shared commitment of institutions, faculty and the public to its value. If academic freedom is to prevail as a norm in American higher education, it is especially important for those in prominent leadership positions to defend the right of controversial speakers within the academic community. If universities in the twenty-first century lose some of the insularity that they enjoyed in the second half of the twentieth century, they will become more vulnerable to the whims of public opinion and the desires of public officials.[23] If faculty members and

cumbent upon universities and their leaders to protect the freedom to assemble and debate, explore questions and test ideas. That can be difficult in a time of stress and pain, but it is never more important," http://www.aaup.org/statements/SpchState/9-11stmt.htm (visited Mar. 12, 2002).

[22]The authors were unable to discover any public opinion polling data dealing specifically with academic freedom since 9/11. However, other polls show Americans' willingness to restrict freedom as a means of preventing future terrorist attacks. For example, a *New York Times* poll taken Sept. 13–14, 2001, showed that 74% of respondents believed that "Americans will have to give up some of their personal freedoms in order to make the country safe from terrorist attacks," httl://www.pollingreport.com/terror6.htm (visited March 30, 2002) According to a poll by Princeton Survey Research, taken Jan. 31–Feb. 1, 2002, 23% of Americans said that the Bush Administration had not gone far enough in restricting U.S. civil liberties in response to terrorism, while 59% said the situation is being handled about right. Only 12% of respondents said the government has gone too far. Roper Center at University of Connecticut, Public Opinion Online, http://web.lexis-nexis.com/universe (accession number 0396551, visited Mar. 30, 2002).

[23]Roger Bowen, then president of the State University of New York at New Paltz, argued in an essay in the *Chronicle of Higher Education* that market pressures are

students become afraid to speak their minds, especially when they have doubts about government policy, the role of the university as a forum for the development and exchange of ideas will be diminished. If the foundation of academic freedom is worn away through institutions' failure to vigorously protect it, the concept will lose its strength as a bulwark of intellectual inquiry.

HISTORICAL AND PHILOSOPHICAL ROOTS OF ACADEMIC FREEDOM

The American Association of University Professors has been the most vigilant guardian of academic freedom at colleges and universities. Formed in 1915, the AAUP made the articulation of a theory for its claims of academic freedom one of its initial goals.[24] The result was the AAUP's 1915 General Report of the Committee on Academic Freedom and Academic Tenure.[25] The 1915 Declaration drew on sources as diverse as the libertarian ideals of J.S. Mill and "Pauline notions of stewardship."[26] It expressly built on prevailing German notions of *lehrfreiheit*—the freedom of the teacher to teach—and *lernfreiheit*—the freedom of the student to learn.[27] According to Metzger, the 1915 Declaration was the first authoritative statement of American notions of academic freedom.[28] It was built on the concept of institutional neutrality and articulated a three-part vision: Academic freedom consisted of the freedom of faculty to teach, to do research and to talk and write on matters outside her or his discipline.[29]

---

increasingly forcing university administrators to respond to academic issues as corporate managers. Roger W. Bowen, *The New Battle Between Political and Economic Cultures*, CHRON. OF HIGHER EDUC., June 22, 2001, at 14. Bowen later resigned from the university to become director of the Milwaukee Public Museum. *Embattled President of SUNY Campus Leaves to Head Milwaukee Museum*, CHRON. OF HIGHER EDUC., Sept. 7, 2001, at 30. *Cf.* Irving Louis Horowitz, *Culture, Politics and McCarthyism: A Retrospective From the Trenches*, 22 WM. MITCHELL L. REV. 357 (1996)(arguing that the primary impact of McCarthyism was to drive a wedge between American culture and politics especially within American higher education institutions).

[24]The AAUP's Committee on Academic Freedom and Academic Tenure was formed in 1915. Metzger, *supra* note 3, at 13–14.

[25]1915 Declaration, *supra* note 3.

[26]Metzger, *supra* note 3, at 13–14.

[27]1915 Declaration, *supra* note 3. The AAUP's position on the academic freedom of students always has been ambiguous. The goal of the AAUP was certainly more focused on the interests of teachers.

[28]Metzger, *supra* note 3 at 13.

[29]*Id.* at 14–15.

In some ways the 1915 Declaration reads as a manifesto.[30] It is a statement of philosophy and not a set of rules. With the 1915 Declaration as a blueprint, the AAUP began two parallel sets of activities that ensured that its vision of academic freedom would become predominant. It sought to establish relationships with other academic organizations such as the American Association of Universities and the American Association of Colleges, as well as other learned societies.[31] It also began a process of investigating and reporting on the complaints of individual faculty members regarding alleged infringements of academic freedom.[32] As the AAUP sought to build relationships with other academic groups, however, it needed a set of agreed principles of academic freedom.[33] This pressure lead the AAUP to re-articulate the basis and scope of academic freedom. The resulting document is the 1940 Statement of Principles.[34]

The 1940 Statement contains three core provisions that also generally correspond with this three-part vision of research, teaching and service responsibilities of most university professors:

a. Teachers are entitled to full freedom in research and in the publication of the results, subject to the adequate performance of their other academic duties; but research for pecuniary re-

---

[30]Metzger describes the 1915 Declaration thusly: "The term [principles] was a misnomer, not because the authors commingled policies and precepts, ... but because, despite the obvious need for brevity, they refused to reduce their value judgments to a few unargued propositions. Theirs, they felt, was to reason why, and their reasoning, which borrowed from intellectual history and social philosophy as well as from practical ethics, was intended to provide a rationale founded on a coherent, if not elaborately embroidered, theory." Metzger, *supra* note 3, at 13.

[31]*Id.* at 17–18. Metzger details the efforts of the AAUP to establish these relationships. It was unsuccessful at forging a relationship with the AAU while, according to Metzger, the 1940 Statement was the result of a pact between the AAC and the AAUP. In any case, today more than 100 organizations and learned societies have endorsed the 1940 Statement of Principles. American Association of University Professors, http://www.aaup.org/statements/Redbook/1940stat.htm (visited Mar. 26, 2002).

[32]*Id.* at 16. Today investigations of the AAUP are regularly reported on in the organization's publication, *Academe* (formerly the *AAUP Bulletin*) and on its Web site. The list of censured organizations is also listed on the Web site. American Association of University Professors, http://www.aaup.org/Com-a/Censure.htm (visited Mar. 26, 2002).

[33]This is an exceedingly elliptical description of the negotiation process that led to the 1940 Statement of Principles. *See generally* Metzger, *supra* note 3, for an exhaustive history of the process leading to the 1940 Statement.

[34]American Association of University Professors, *1940 Statement of Principles on Academic Freedom and Tenure*, http://www.aaup.org/statements/Redbook/1940stat.htm (visited March 18, 2002). *See also Appendix B: 1940 Statement of Principles on Academic Freedom and Tenure,* 53 L. & CONTEMP. PROBS. 407 (1990).

turn should be based upon an understanding with the authorities of the institution.

b. Teachers are entitled to freedom in the classroom in discussing their subject, but they should be careful not to introduce into their teaching controversial matter that has no relation to their subject. Limitations of academic freedom because of religious or other aims of the institution should be clearly stated in writing at the time of the appointment.

c. College and university teachers are citizens, members of a learned profession, and officers of an educational institution. When they speak or write as citizens, they should be free from institutional censorship or discipline, but their special position in the community imposes special obligations. As scholars and educational officers, they should remember that the public may judge their profession and their institution by their utterances. Hence they should at all times be accurate, should exercise appropriate restraint, should show respect for the opinions of others, and should make every effort to indicate that they are not speaking for the institution.[35]

These provisions are based on the explicit assumptions of the drafters that "institutions of higher education exist not for themselves but for the 'common good'; that academic freedom is 'essential' to that purpose; that academic tenure is 'essential' to academic freedom no less than to academic job security; and that 'academic freedom carries with it duties correlative with rights.'"[36]

The success of the AAUP at obtaining the support of other academic organizations for its statements regarding academic freedom, and the ongoing publication of the reports of its investigations and censures, has been responsible, in part, for the primacy of the AAUP's vision and has been the engine driving the development of a shared understanding of academic freedom. Theoretically, an organization can ignore AAUP actions. And, while some institutions have not responded to AAUP criticism, most respond because they do not wish to place themselves outside the community of colleges and universities. The list of censured institutions is remarkably short—fifty-one.[37] Thus norms, of academic freedom have been en-

---

[35]*Id.*

[36]Metzger, *supra* note 3, at 8 (summarizing the preamble of the 1940 Statement of Principles).

[37]*Id.*

forced through a complex set of relationships and commitments and rarely are enforced by courts.

CONTRACT PROTECTION OF ACADEMIC FREEDOM

While we argue that the preservation of academic freedom on campus is largely the result of a "compact" of sorts, or a set of shared understandings among faculty, administrators and the public, it would be a mistake to ignore the ways in which norms of academic freedom are enforced by courts. Academic freedom has both contractual and free speech components that have received protection from courts.

Many universities' faculty handbooks or other official documents contain express protections of academic freedom. In some cases, these documents expressly reference or incorporate the 1940 Statement of Principles. In other cases, the documents contain original statements of commitment to academic freedom. Under prevailing contract law in many states, these official university pronouncements become part of an employee's contract with the university.[38] Other cases have recognized that a right to academic freedom can be based on the custom and tradition of a particular university.[39]

The protection afforded academic freedom by contract law is not clearly defined. Contract protections are limited by the language of university documents dealing with academic freedom and by the ability under state law to make those documents part of an employment contract. Certainly academic freedom's continuing tender in academia is not attributable to its protection by contracts. Rather its currency is attributable to our cultural notions of the university and the willingness of university faculty, administrators and students to adhere to the ideal of academic freedom.

FIRST AMENDMENT PROTECTION OF ACADEMIC FREEDOM

While the core values of academic freedom are secured though individual and institutional commitment to the AAUP's 1940 Statement, American courts have found a nexus between the ideal of academic freedom and rights of free speech protected in the First Amendment. Yet, despite the fact that the Court has referred to academic freedom as "a special concern of the First Amendment,"[40] the

[38] *See generally*, Jim Jackson, *Express and Implied Contractual Rights to Academic Freedom in the United States*, 22 HAMLINE L. REV. 467 (1999).

[39] *Id.* at 483–88.

[40] Keyishian v. Bd. of Regents, 385 U.S. 589, 603 (1967).

scope of the First Amendment protection afforded academic speech is ambiguous at best.[41]

In his comprehensive history of academic freedom in the Supreme Court, William Van Alstyne traces the first express association between academic freedom and the First Amendment to *Adler v. Board of Education*[42] and *Wieman v. Updegraff*.[43] The two cases, decided during the Court's 1951–52 term, dealt with state regulations arising from the Cold War. *Adler* involved New York's Feinberg Law,[44] which required that any person espousing the use of violence to alter the form of U.S. government be removed from public employment. Although the Court upheld the state law, Justice William O. Douglas dissented, reasoning that the law unreasonably infringed on the academic freedom of public school teachers.[45] *Wieman* was a challenge to the constitutionality of a state statute requiring that state employees take an oath disclaiming affiliation with a subversive organization as a condition of employment.[46] In contrast to *Adler*, a majority struck down the statute, on grounds that it infringed associational rights of state employees. Justice Felix Frankfurter wrote separately, arguing that the oath would also have a pernicious effect on the academic freedom of teachers.[47]

These early cases set the stage for a trio of Supreme Court decisions during the 1950s and 1960s that defined the Court's willingness to provide First Amendment protection to teachers based on grounds of academic freedom. In *Sweezy v. New Hampshire*[48] the Court visited the question of academic freedom and the First Amendment in yet another challenge to the constitutionality of Cold War anti-subversive legislation. The case involved the contempt prosecution of a University of New Hampshire professor who refused to provide details of his lectures and political associations in answer to questions by the state attorney general as part

[41]J. Peter Byrne, *Academic Freedom: A "Special Concern of the First Amendment,"* 99 YALE L. J. 251, 252 (1989)("Attempts to understand the scope and foundation of a constitutional guarantee of academic freedom, however, generally result in paradox or confusion.").

[42]342 U.S. 485 (1952).

[43]344 U.S. 183 (1952).

[44]Named for a leading proponent of the legislation, these statutes were aimed at weeding "subversives" out of public employment. Van Alstyne, *supra* note 2, at 105.

[45]342 U.S. at 509 (Douglas, J., dissenting).

[46]344 U.S. at 191. This short history of the First Amendment aspects of academic freedom is based on the more detailed and thoughtful history in Van Alstyne, *supra* note 2. *See also* Byrne, *supra* note 41, at 288–299.

[47]344 U.S. at 195 (Frankfurter, J., concurring).

[48]354 U.S. 234 (1957).

of a state anti-subversive investigation. Justice Frankfurter defined the connection between free speech and academic freedom in his concurring opinion, reasoning that the examination of the content of Sweezy's lectures violated rights of academic freedom rights by the First Amendment. Frankfurter wrote, "When weighed against the grave harm [to academic freedom] resulting from governmental intrusion into the intellectual life of a university, [ordinary justifications] for compelling a witness to discuss the contents of his lecture [appear] grossly inadequate."[49] If the professor was subject to prosecution for the content of his lectures, Frankfurter reasoned that the chilling effect on the continued free exchange of ideas within the university would be immeasurable.[50]

Frankfurter's reasoning in *Sweezy* is interesting. His analysis appears to be rooted in the government's intrusion into the university as an institution; he characterizes the government's action as an intrusion into the "intellectual life of a university" not as an intrusion into the free speech and association rights of a professor.[51] Yet the case involved an individual faculty member, not the University of New Hampshire. Moreover, the university, as a public institution, was a governmental entity. Furthermore, Frankfurter's conclusions, based on the general value to society of free academic inquiry, do not address the scope of First Amendment inquiry. Frankfurter's grand but unspecific conclusion is that a free society depends on free universities, and that "this means the exclusion of governmental intervention in the intellectual life of a university."[52]

The Court recognized the link between free speech and academic freedom for the first time in 1967 in *Keyishian v. Board of Regents*,[53] striking down the provisions of New York's Feinberg law, previously upheld in *Adler*. Writing for the majority, Justice William Brennan reasoned:

> [A]cademic freedom ... is of transcendent value to all of us and not merely to the teachers concerned. That freedom is therefore a special concern of the First Amendment, which does not tolerate laws that case a pall of orthodoxy over the classroom. ... The classroom is particularly the marketplace of ideas. The Nation's future depends upon lead-

[49]*Id.* at 261 (Frankfurter, J., concurring).

[50]The characterization is Professor Van Alstyne's. Van Alstyne, *supra* note 2, at 111.

[51]354 U.S. at 261 (Frankfurter, J., concurring).

[52]*Id.* at 262 (Frankfurter, J., concurring).

[53]385 U.S. 589 (1967).

> ers trained through wide exposure to that robust exchange of ideas which discovers truth out of a multitude of tongues, [rather] than through any kind of authoritative selection.[54]

The *Keyeshian* Court relied on the reasoning of *Sweezy* in its analysis, and, as in Frankfurter's opinion in *Sweezy*, reverted to grand conclusions and avoided specific analysis. While Justice Brennan characterized academic freedom as a "transcendent value,"[55] the opinion does not shed additional light on the relationship between academic freedom and the First Amendment.

The year after *Keyishian*, Justice Douglas wrote the majority opinion in *Whitehill v. Elkins*,[56] striking down an oath similar to that in *Wieman* on express academic freedom grounds. Continuing the invocation of academic freedom without specific analysis, the court concluded, "The continuing surveillance which this type of law places on teachers is hostile to academic freedom. ... The restraints on conscientious teachers are obvious."[57]

The promise of a well-articulated First Amendment basis for academic freedom represented by these cases has not been borne out by the Court. It has not addressed the First Amendment and academic freedom in any detail in the years since *Keyeshian* and *Whitehill*. Opinions invoking academic freedom are most often explained by other lines of analysis.[58] One result of the paucity of authority is that confusing distinctions exist between individual academic freedom—the freedom of individual faculty and researchers to speak and teach without institutional intervention—and institutional academic freedom—the right of colleges and universities to be free from intervention of the state.[59] The AAUP's 1940 Statement is primarily a statement of the rights of individual professors to academic freedom; the First Amendment cases, while recogniz-

[54]*Id.* at 603.

[55]*Id.*

[56]389 U.S. 54 (1967).

[57]*Id.* at 59 (citing *Sweezy*, 354 U.S. at 250). *Cf.* Badgett v. Bullit, 377 U.S. 360 (1964)(striking down two anti-subversive oath provisions that applied to university teachers on First Amendment grounds but not on academic freedom grounds).

[58]Van Alstyne discusses the post-*Keyeshian* cases in detail with regard to the elaboration of an academic freedom and First Amendment doctrine. *See, e.g.*, Van Alstyne, *supra* note 2, at 118–138.

[59]*See*, Walter P. Metzger, *Profession and Constitution: Two Definitions of Academic Freedom in America*, 66 TEX. L. REV. 1265 (1988); David M. Rabban, *A Functional Analysis of "Individual" and "Institutional" Academic Freedom Under the First Amendment*, 53 L. & CONTEMP. PROBS. 227 (1990).

ing the individual aspects of academic freedom, deal primarily with institutional freedom.[60]

In addition to being ambiguous, the potentially broad reach of First Amendment cases may be limited by the development of the "public employee doctrine." The doctrine, deriving from early cases involving free speech and public employees, including *Adler*, has defined the scope of free speech rights of public employees, including, arguably, teachers and faculty members at public institutions.[61] The Court has held that the free speech rights of an employee speaking about matters of public concern must be balanced against the government's interest in the efficient operation of the governmental entity involved.[62] Interestingly enough, although the primary modern case addressing this doctrine, *Pickering v. Board of Education*, involved speech by a public school teacher, the Court did not rely on notions of academic freedom for its conclusion that the teacher's free speech rights were infringed by the school district.[63] In fact, the Court cited *Keyishian* and *Whitehill* only for the proposition that public employees do not shed the free speech rights enjoyed by all citizens simply because they are in the public's employ.[64]

While the *Pickering* Court concluded that the teacher's free speech rights had been impermissibly invaded, the decision established a framework in which public employers could regulate the speech of public employees to a greater degree than if those individuals were not public employees. The test balanced the government's interest in the efficient operation of public services and in not having those services disrupted against the speech of the public employee. The potential disruptiveness of a public employee's speech must out-

---

[60]*See* Rabban, *supra* note 59, at 229. One commentator has argued that only the institutional aspect of academic freedom is protected by the Supreme Court. *See* Byrne, *supra* note 41, at 312–322.

[61]*See* Van Alstyne, *supra* note 2, at 83–84 and 105–06. Van Alstyne traces the "bad tendency" cases to nineteenth century First Amendment jurisprudence. *See, e.g.,* the opinion of Justice Oliver Wendell Holmes in *McAuliffe v. Mayor of New Bedford*, 29 N.E. 517, 518 (1892), addressing the free speech argument of a police officer discharged for criticizing the police department:

> The petitioner may have a constitutional right to talk politics, but he has no constitutional right to be a policeman. There are few employments for hire in which the servant does not agree to suspend his constitutional right of free speech as well as of idleness, by the implied terms of his contract. The servant cannot complain, as he takes the employment on the terms that are offered him.

[62]*See* Waters v. Churchill, 511 U.S. 661 (1994); Connick v. Meyers, 461 U.S. 138 (1983); Pickering v. Bd. of Educ, 391 U.S. 563 (1968).

[63]391 U.S. at 564–68.

[64]*Id.* at 568.

weigh the value of that speech.[65] Finally, the Court has held that the government must act to avoid the disruption in pubic services and not as retaliation against the speech itself.[66]

The public employee doctrine, and *Pickering* in particular, raise questions about the extent of First Amendment protection for academic freedom.[67] While the doctrine certainly recognizes that the speech of public employees is protected by the First Amendment, it nonetheless appears to treat the speech of teachers no differently from the speech of other public employees. It may be that *Pickering* does not reach to the speech of college and university teachers[68] or that it only applies to the speech of teachers outside the areas of the classroom and scholarly pursuits.[69] While the latter limitation would be inconsistent with the AAUP's conception of academic freedom,[70] it would leave intact the reasoning of *Sweezy*, *Keyishian* and *Whitehill*.

The connection between the First Amendment and academic freedom is appealing. At first blush the relationship seems obvious. Certainly the First Amendment is rooted in many of the same values that inform academic freedom—those of free association, freedom of thought and inquiry and freedom of speech. Broad generalizations regarding the importance of free thought to free societies, such as Frankfurter's statements in *Sweezy*, seem undebatable on their face. Despite this apparent relationship, however, there are both structural and theoretical limitations on the promise of the First Amendment as a bulwark against incursions on academic freedom.

Structurally, the First Amendment can only reach governmental incursions on academic freedom. *Sweezy*, *Keyishian* and *Whitehill* all involved attempts by state government to interfere with academic speech. Yet many of the instances we detail later in this paper involve interference with academic inquiry by private entities or actions by a

---

[65]*Connick*, 461 U.S. at 147–148.

[66]*Waters*, 511 U.S. at 680.

[67]*See generally*, Matthew W. Finkin, *Intramural Speech, Academic Freedom and the First Amendment*, 66 TEX. L. REV. 1323 (1988). Finkin's article was part of a symposium, and the two shorter comments on it are also helpful. *See* Mark G. Yudof, *Intramural Musings on Academic Freedom: A Reply to Professor Finkin*, 66 TEX. L REV. 1351 (1988), and Paul Brest, *Protecting Academic Freedom Through the First Amendment: Raising the Unanswered Questions*, 66 TEX. L. REV. 1359 (1988).

[68]*See, e.g.*, Peter E. Barber, *Recent Decision—Bishop v. Aranov: "No Talking in Class!": Does the Elementery Adage Apply to University Professors?* 44 ALA. L. REV. 211, 230 (1992).

[69]For detailed discussion of the scope of *Pickering* and its relationship to academic freedom, see the sources cited in *supra* note 67.

[70]Part (c) of the 1940 Statement of Principles expressly protects the external speech of teachers on matters of public concern. *See* text accompanying *supra* note 35.

university itself against its faculty member based on the faculty member's speech. Because a constitutional claim requires some action by a state actor, the First Amendment would not be implicated directly where a private university takes disciplinary action against a faculty member based on the person's speech[71] and yet, such action would raise academic freedom issues.

Moreover, the striking failure of the Court to extend its reasoning in the years since *Sweezy, Keyishian* and *Whitehill* were decided, may indicate that the reach of those decisions is limited. They might be characterized as more a product of their times than the beginnings of a constitutionally based theory of academic freedom. All three cases arose out of the sweeping and often clumsy attempts of states to reach and regulate perceived subversive activity during the Cold War. Given this context, it may be that the cases really stand only for the limited proposition that the state may not use universities as a weapon in an overbroad and ill-defined fishing expedition. Frankfurter hints at such a theory when he focuses on the institutional needs of a university to make its own decisions about the nature and scope of academic inquiry.[72] The constitutional protection of academic freedom may not extend beyond this situation to interference by state-supported universities and schools into the academic freedom of their faculties.

It is also not clear what sorts of governmental purposes would support regulations that interfere with academic freedom. Frankfurter's opinion in *Sweezy* and the majority opinions in *Keyishian* and *Whitehill* each focus on the weakness of the government's purpose. In *Sweezy*, Frankfurter reasoned that Sweezy's academic freedom rights could not be "encroached upon on the basis of so meagre [sic] a countervailing interest of the State as may be argumentatively found in the remote, shadowy threat to the security of New Hampshire ... ."[73] Writing for the majority in *Keyishian*, Douglas concluded that "the very intricacy of the plan and the uncertainty as to the scope of its proscriptions make it a highly efficient *in terrorem* mechanism."[74] The majority in *Whitehill* concluded: "Precision and

[71]*See* Byrne, *supra* note 41, at 299–301.

[72]Frankfurter extensively quotes a plea for academic freedom at South African universities which concludes, in part, that the "'four essential freedoms' of a university" are the freedoms "to determine for itself on academic grounds who may teach, what may be taught, how it shall be taught, and who may be admitted to study." Sweezy v. New Hampshire, 354 U.S. 234, 263 (1957)(Frankfurter, J., concurring).

[73]354 U.S. at 265 (Frankfurter, J., concurring).

[74]385 U.S. 589, 601 (1967).

clarity are not present. Rather we find an overbreadth that makes possible oppressive or capricious application as regimes change."[75]

Narrowly tailored regulations supported by perceived needs to foster institutional independence and academic purposes might more easily survive scrutiny. Reading the academic freedom decisions together with the public employee cases leads to exactly such a conclusion. On the one hand, *Keyishian* holds that direct governmental intervention requires specific, narrowly tailored regulations based on compelling state interests. On the other hand, *Pickering* upholds university or school regulations supported by concerns of the school as an employer in maintaining the efficient operation of public services. The Court's failure to address academic freedom concerns in its public employee cases involving teachers also can be explained both by the fact that *Sweezy*, *Keyishian* and *Whitehill* are applicable only in a limited context and by the fact that narrowly tailored, specific regulations regarding employment must be scrutinized under some analytical framework other than academic freedom.

In the end, as attractive as the academic freedom/First Amendment argument is on the surface, faculty who look to the Constitution to protect their rights to academic freedom are likely to be disappointed. The cases simply do not provide a coherent framework for the enforcement of academic freedom rights, particularly by individual faculty members whose college or university seeks to restrict that faculty members' speech. And, the First Amendment cases do not directly reach academic freedom issues in private universities.

UNIVERSITY RESPONSE TO PREVIOUS NATIONAL CRISES

Responses to previous national crises have often led to infringements on academic freedom. Interestingly, these responses have differed in character from crisis to crisis—reflecting the unique concerns and social issues of the time. During World War I, colleges and universities fired radical teachers espousing pacifist views.[76] For

---

[75]389U.S. 54, 62 (1967).

[76]One of the most well-documented cases was that of economics professor Scott Nearing, dismissed by the University of Pennsylvania in 1915 and hired by the University of Toledo, only to be fired in 1917—eleven days after the United States entered the war—for his opposition to the war. Another was William A. Schaper, a political science professor at the University of Minnesota, fired in September of 1917 for "his expressed unwillingness to aid the United States in the present war." *See* ELLEN W. SCHRECKER, NO IVORY TOWER: MCCARTHYISM AND THE UNIVERSITIES 19–22 (1986). At the time, the AAUP declined to support the claims to academic freedom of these individuals. *See* David M. Rabin, *Free Speech in Progressive Social*

a few years after World War II, there was what one historian called "a brief, and now forgotten, efflorescence of political radicalism at many of the nation's colleges and universities."[77] However, once the Cold War between the United States and the Soviet Union deepened, universities renewed their attempts to root out alleged subversives on campus. The hearings of the House Un-American Activities Committee in 1947 and the Permanent Subcommittee on Investigations of the Senate Committee on Government Operations (chaired by Senator Joseph McCarthy of Wisconsin) in 1950 gave license to state legislators, college trustees and university regents to pursue similar investigations in their own states.[78] During the McCarthy period, the primary threat to academic freedom was the imposition by government of loyalty oaths and other schemes intended to weed out suspected communists in public higher education institutions.[79]

The context of academic freedom issues changed significantly after 1960. During the 1960s, attempts to restrict speech were directed primarily at students protesting the Vietnam War or agitating for civil rights.[80] Some of this agitation wound its way to the courts in a context that raised academic freedom issues. In *Healy v. James,*[81] a case overturning a college's refusal to officially recognize a local chapter of Students for a Democratic Society, Justice Lewis Powell began his opinion with the statement that "[w]e break no new constitutional ground in reaffirming this Nation's dedication to safeguard-

---

Thought, 74 TEX L. REV. 951, 963 (1996) (reviewing AAUP president John Dewey's views on free speech).

77SHRECKER, *supra* note 76, at 84.

78Shrecker writes that the federal government's demand for loyalty oaths "acted as a catalyst" for universities to seek to expel suspected Communists. *Id.* at 93 *See also* LIONEL S. LEWIS, COLD WAR ON CAMPUS: A STUDY OF THE POLITICS OF ORGANIZATION CONTROL (1988), and JANE SANDERS, COLD WAR ON THE CAMPUS: ACADEMIC FREEDOM AT THE UNIVERSITY OF WASHINGTON, 1946–64 (1979).

79*See* Keyishian v. Bd. of Regents, 385 U.S. 589, 592 (1967) (challenging New York's Feinberg Law); Whitehill v. Elkins, 389 U.S. 54, 55–56 (1967) (challenging the teachers oath enacted by Maryland as part of its legislative crackdown on subversive organizations); Sweezy v. New Hampshire, 354 U.S. 234, 236 (1957) (challenging a subpoena for testimony before a New Hampshire legislative committee investigating subversive organizations). These three cases resulted from such Cold War era legislation.

80Certainly faculty members were involved in critiques of U.S. policy in Vietnam. *See, e.g.,* Franklin v. Leland Stanford Junior University, 218 Cal. Rptr. 228 (Cal. App. 1985) (appeal arising from professor's 1971 call for students to take over university computer lab to protest the Vietnam War). However, controversy over their activism was not led by their universities, and governmental actions to quell their protests were not directed at universities in particular. As a result, the debates over their activism, and the activism of students, generally, was not framed in terms of academic freedom.

81408 U.S. 169 (1972).

ing academic freedom."[82] The unanimous Court concluded that a ban on an organization because of the ideas it espoused violated the First Amendment.

Much of the ferment regarding academic freedom during this period was, as in *Healy*, directed by students toward university administrations seeking to keep anti-war and civil rights protests from disrupting campus life. Moreover, the traditional defender of academic freedom—the AAUP—was not at the forefront of the battle. Maybe this should not be surprising given the fact that the AAUP's commitment to academic freedom de-emphasized the freedom of students in an academic environment.[83]

DISSENT ON CAMPUS SINCE 9/11

For years preceding the events of September 11, some professors had been speaking and writing about the origins of radical Islamic discontent with U.S. policies in the Middle East.[84] Others responded emotionally and spontaneously, as many Americans did, to the catastrophic events of 9/11.[85] The episodes which prompted the greatest public or institutional response fall into four main categories: spontaneous remarks or classroom exchanges in the days immediately after the terrorist attacks; speeches, articles or public forums in which views critical of U.S. policy were aired; displays of American flags or patriotic slogans that were seen as insensitive to foreign students or religious minorities; and a faculty member's public statements about the Israeli-Palestinian conflict, some more than ten years old, that attracted national public attention when they were re-examined in the aftermath of 9/11. The latter case is unusual because it appears to be the only situation in which a university faculty member's job

[82]*Id.* at 180.

[83]The AAUP omitted the notion of *lernfreiheit*—the German concept of the freedom of the student to learn—from the 1940 Statement. Metzger, *supra* note 3, at 14.

[84]Two of the leading U.S. scholars of Islam are John Esposito of Georgetown University and Bernard Lewis, retired from the University of Pennsylvania. Esposito's books include JOHN ESPOSITO, ISLAM AND POLITICS (1991) and JOHN ESPOSITO, THE ISLAMIC THREAT: MYTH OR REALITY (1992). Lewis is best known for BERNARD LEWIS, THE POLITICAL LANGUAGE OF ISLAM (1988) and BERNARD LEWIS, ISLAM AND THE WEST (1993), a collection of his essays. One of those essays attracted widespread attention after its publication in 1990. *See* Bernard Lewis, *The Roots of Muslim Rage,* ATLANTIC MONTHLY, Sept. 1990, at 47, *available at* http://www.theatlantic.com /issues/90sep/rage.htm (visited May 15, 2002).

[85]As of spring 2002, it was difficult to assess how widespread or long-lasting the effects on campus speech might be. At the national level, however, there has been little change in the tenor of disapproval directed at critics of the war. *See supra* note 15 and accompanying text.

was at stake; in that sense, it may represent the most serious threat to academic freedom as traditionally interpreted in the United States. This is by no means a comprehensive accounting of academic freedom-of-expression controversies since 9/11,[86] however, it reviews some of the ways in which the climate of free and open academic inquiry has been tested on and off campus in the months since the terrorist attacks.[87]

The first category reflects the emotional reaction of students and professors to the attacks on the World Trade Center and the Pentagon, the devastating loss of life and the widespread media coverage of the events. It was in this context that professors at the University of New Mexico and a California community college made statements in the classroom that led to investigations by their respective institutions.

A tasteless joke by Richard M. Berthold, an associate professor of history at the University of New Mexico, prompted disciplinary action and calls for university officials to fire him. Berthold told a class of freshmen the day of the attacks that "anyone who can blow up the Pentagon" gets my vote—a remark for which he apologized. The university's provost, Brian Foster, said that the First Amendment protected Berthold's remarks. Nonetheless, he "failed to act responsibly toward his students at that time," Foster said. As a result, university officials gave Berthold a letter of reprimand, directed him to submit to a post-tenure review and temporarily forbade him to teach any freshman-level classes. Berthold called the reprimand "an entirely appropriate response to the stupidity and callousness of those remarks."[88] After the university's decision was announced, two legislators complained that the punishment should have been more severe. One sought to force the university to fire Berthold by deleting his salary from the state budget, but that measure failed.[89]

[86]The authors relied on press reports, particularly those in the *Chronicle of Higher Education*, as well as the staff of the American Association of University Professors to identify major academic freedom cases that arose after Sept. 11, 2002.

[87]Other threats to the ability of university professors to explore public policy questions are government attempts since 9/11 to restrict access to unclassified records kept by federal agencies. *See* Martin E. Halstuk, *In Review: The Threat to Freedom of Information,* COLUM. JOURNALISM REV., Jan.–Feb. 2002, at 8.

[88]Steve Terrell, *UNM Punishes Professor for His Remark,* SANTA FE NEW MEXICAN, Dec. 11, 2001, at A1. *See also* Robin Wilson & Scott Smallwood, *One Professor Cleared, Another Disciplined Over September 11 Remarks,* CHRON. OF HIGHER EDUC., Jan. 11, 2002, at 12.

[89]Rep. Rob Burpo, R-Albuquerque, said he wanted to send a message to the university. "I think they let the guy off with a slap on the wrist," he reportedly said. Olivier Uyttebrouck, *UNM Prof's Wages Stay In Budget; Legislator Wanted Berthold off Payroll,* ALBUQUERQUE J., Jan. 29, 2002, at D2.

At Orange Coast College in Costa Mesa, California, Muslim students accused political science professor Kenneth W. Hearlson of making derogatory remarks about them in an introduction to government course September 18, 2001. An eleven-week investigation by the Orange County Department of Education, which included a review of tape recordings of Hearlson's lecture, found no evidence to support the charges. The college placed Hearlson on administrative leave during the inquiry but reinstated him before the spring semester began on January 28, 2002. Hearlson complained that college officials had written a letter reprimanding him, but neither he nor the college would release the contents of the letter. The president of an affiliate of the Coast Federation of Educators said her group planned to file a grievance with the college because the letter violated Hearlson's academic freedom.[90] Hearlson said he had spent more than $10,000 in legal fees to retain his job.[91]

Three episodes involving speeches, statements or events are potentially more troubling from an academic freedom perspective because they call into question rights of professors, students and, in one case, a newspaper publisher, to challenge government policy. They involve a newspaper column written by a University of Texas professor, a teach-in on the war at City University of New York and a commencement speech on a California State University campus.

Robert Jensen, a journalism professor at the University of Texas at Austin, wrote a column published September 12, 2001, by the *Houston Chronicle*, in which he suggested that U.S. policy may have indirectly caused the terrorist attacks. While denouncing the terrorists who carried out the attacks, he wrote, "My anger on this day is directed not only at individuals who engineered the September 11 tragedy but at those who have held power in the United States and have engineered attacks on civilians every bit as tragic."[92] The university's president, Larry R. Faulkner, responded with a letter to the editor of the same newspaper, distancing the institution from Jensen, calling him a "fountain of undiluted foolishness on issues of

---

[90]*See* Wilson & Smallwood, *supra* note 88, at 12.

[91]In his first class after the suspension ended, Hearlson, wearing an American flag pin on his lapel, declared: "This is America. We have a constitutional right to be stupid and to offend people." Jeff Gottlieb, *Contrary OCC Professor Back; Students Seem Oblivious to Bait,* L.A. TIMES, Jan. 29, 2002, pt. 2 (Orange County Edition), at 3.

[92]The full text of Jensen's essay is available on several Web sites, including the *Houston Chronicle's*: http://www.chron.com/cs/CDA/story.hts/editorial/1047072. *See also* http://uts.cc.utexas.edu/~rjensen/freelance/attack1.htm (visited Mar. 29, 2002).

public policy," but defending his right to express his opinion.[93] After Jensen's letter was published, letters and phone calls to university officials sought the professor's dismissal, but Faulkner responded that "it would be far more damaging to the university to undertake to penalize someone for free expression."[94] Jensen had not been subjected to any official disciplinary action, though he feared that the president's remarks might deter others on his campus from speaking out.[95] Other University of Texas faculty members expressed concern about the president's response. "The faculty felt there was a very clear message that if you stick your neck out, we [the university] will disown you," said Dana L. Cloud, an associate professor of communication studies.[96]

At City University of New York, the faculty organized a "teach-in" October 2, 2001, to examine the causes of the terrorist attacks. Several professors criticized U.S. foreign policy, prompting Chancellor Matthew Goldstein to publicly denounce the professors who presented these views. "I have no sympathy for the voices of those who make lame excuses for the attacks on the World Trade Center and the Pentagon based on ideological or historical circumstances," Goldstein declared.[97] Two days later, the university's trustees drafted a resolution condemning the event as seditious.[98] Goldstein's actions were particularly troubling because he spoke in his official capacity.[99]

---

[93] *Jensen's Views His Own*, HOUSTON CHRON. on-line edition, http://www.chron.com/cs/CDA/story.hts/editorial/1053207#jensen (posted Sept. 19, 2002; visited May 19, 2002).

[94] Ron Nissimov, *UT Professor Expected Criticism From Letter; Threat of Backlash Keeps Others From Speaking Out*, HOUSTON CHRON., Sept. 14, 2001, at A13.

[95] Jensen wrote in January, "I didn't take it personally that my boss didn't like my ideas. My concern about his broadside was the possible chilling effect it would have on others, especially untenured professors and students." *Four Months Later, No Regrets for Writing Against U.S. Policy,* HOUSTON CHRON. on-line edition, http://www.chron.com/cs/CDA/story.hts/editorial/outlook/1215826 (visited May 19, 2002).

[96] Robin Wilson and Ana Marie Cox, *Terrorist Attacks Put Academic Freedom to the Test,* CHRON. OF HIGHER EDUC., Oct. 5, 2001, at 12.

[97] Anemona Hartocollis, *CUNY Chief Repudiates Forum Remarks*, N.Y. TIMES, Oct. 4, 2001, at D3.

[98] Robin Wilson, *CUNY Chancellor, Trustees Denounce Professors Who Criticized U.S. Policy After Attacks,* CHRON. OF HIGHER EDUC., Oct. 5, 2001, on-line edition, http://chronicle.com/daily/2001/10/2001100502n.htm (visited Mar. 31, 2002). The article noted that the trustees and chancellor did not attend the event but based their response on accounts of the teach-in published in the *New York Post.*

[99] Martin Snyder, director of planning and development for the American Association of University Professors, commented: "When the chief administrator abandons institutional neutrality and officially counters faculty views on matters beyond the running of the university, she or he sends a message, intended or not, that the free exchange of ideas and the right to dissent from the majority view may entail a very high price. The potential for retaliation is real, especially for untenured faculty

More than three months after the terrorist attacks, an audience at California State University in Sacramento booed commencement speaker Janis Besler Heaphy, preventing her from finishing her speech. Heaphy, publisher and president of the *Sacramento Bee*, questioned some of the government's responses to 9/11, including racial profiling, secret military tribunals and attempts by U.S. officials to manipulate the press. "No one argues the validity and need for both retaliation and security. But to what lengths are we willing to go to achieve them?" she asked. Her remarks prompted booing and synchronized clapping from the crowd in the arena. After the university's president was unable to quiet the disturbance—which witnesses said came primarily from sections reserved for family members of graduates—Heaphy halted her speech.[100] The *Bee* later published the text, which urged students: "Be inquisitive. Remember, asking questions about government policies isn't disloyal. It's your duty."[101]

Not all campus controversies derived from criticisms of U.S. policies. Some arose as a result of verbal or visual displays of grief, patriotism or national unity—sometimes without any overt political intention. Typical of these was that surrounding Margaret Post, a secretary at the College of the Holy Cross in Worcester, Massachusetts, a friend of a passenger on one of the hijacked flights. Post hung a flag in her office three days after the attack, but her department chair, Royce Singleton, asked her to remove it. When she refused, Singleton removed the flag and placed it on her desk. The college received telephone calls of complaint after the episode was reported in local newspapers. Singleton apologized and allowed Post to place a small flag on her desk.[102]

In September, Charles H. Fairbanks, a professor of international relations at Johns Hopkins University, said at a public forum that he would "bet anyone here a Koran" that the United States would be unable to capture suspected terrorist Osama Bin Laden. Asked who might be responsible for the September 11 attacks, Fairbanks mentioned Iraq, Pakistan and the Palestinian authority, adding "Unfor-

members." Martin Snyder, *Academic Freedom in a Time of Crisis,* ACADEME, Jan.–Feb. 2002, on-line edition, http://www.aaup.org/publications/academe/02jf/02jfSOTP.htm (visited May 19, 2002).

[100]Geofrey Mohan, *Graduation Speech Riles Sacramento,* L.A. TIMES, Dec. 20, 2001, pt. 2, at 1.

[101]The *Bee* published the text Dec. 22, 2001, at B7, *available at* http://www.sacbee.com/content/opinion/story/1339967p-1409462c.html (visited March 30, 2002).

[102]David Abel, *America Prepares Domestic Impact; Campuses See a Downside to Unity; Civil Rights Stifled, Some Professors Say*, BOSTON GLOBE, Oct. 6, 2001, at 7.

tunately, Palestinians hate us and that's a painful fact." A woman in the audience accused him of attempting to stir up hate against Muslims. Fairbanks apologized for his remark about the Koran. Less than a week later, Stephen F. Szabo, dean of the Paul H. Nitze School of Advanced International Studies, demoted Fairbanks to a research professor, saying he was unqualified to direct the Central Asia-Caucasus Institute.[103] After a column mentioning Fairbanks' situation appeared in *The New Republic* magazine, Szabo reinstated Fairbanks to his administrative position.[104]

The case of Sami Al-Arian, a computer science professor at the University of South Florida, is troubling for several reasons. Al-Arian, who was hired by USF in 1986, is the only U.S. faculty member to face dismissal as a result of 9/11—yet the sequence of events that jeopardize his job began eleven years ago.[105] Sensitive to charges it might be restricting academic freedom, the university has sought to rationalize its decision by asserting that it merely wants to end a controversy that has disrupted the campus. The American Association of University Professors considered the case serious enough to dispatch a three-member team to meet with the university's president.[106]

Al-Arian has a long history of controversy, which has undoubtedly led university officials to be sensitive to his public statements.[107] The University of South Florida suspended him with pay in 1996 after federal agencies suspected that an institute he founded, the World Islamic Studies Enterprise, was connected to terrorists in the Middle East. The government never filed criminal charges against Al-Arian, and the university reinstated him in 1998.[108] His recent troubles began when he was invited to appear on a television interview program, "The O'Reilly Factor," September 26, 2001. Host Bill O'Reilly asked

[103]Peter Beinart, *TRB from Washington: Talk Show*, NEW REPUBLIC, Oct. 22, 2001, at 6.

[104]Piper Fogg, *At Johns Hopkins U., Brouhaha Brings Vacillation*, CHRON. OF HIGHER EDUC., Oct. 26, 2001, at A8.

[105]*Sami Al-Arian: Career and Controversy at South Florida*, CHRON. OF HIGHER EDUC., Feb. 8, 2002, at A11.

[106]The AAUP decided to investigate after determining that the case "raised issues of academic freedom, tenure and due process that are of basic concern to the academic community and are incumbent on us to address." Graham Brink, *Investigator: USF Chief Wavering on Al-Arian's Fate*, ST. PETERSBURG TIMES, Apr. 26, 2002, at 1B.

[107]The university, however, gave some support to the World Islamic Studies Enterprise, a group that Al-Arian formed in 1991 to prompt dialogue between Muslims and other intellectuals. *See Sami Al-Arian*, *supra* note 105, at A11.

[108]Susan Aschoff, *Professor Back at USF After Suspension*, ST. PETERSBURG TIMES, Aug. 26, 1998, at 3B.

Al-Arian about a speech he made in 1988 in which he said, "Jihad is our path. Victory to Islam. Death to Israel." Al-Arian said his remarks were taken out of context. The day after the program was broadcast, the University of South Florida started receiving telephone calls and e-mail messages in protest.[109]

The university responded by placing Al-Arian on paid leave and telling him not to return to campus. In a hastily called meeting on December 19, the USF Board of Trustees voted 12–1 to recommend his dismissal. Richard A. Beard III, chairman of the trustees, said circumstantial evidence of Al-Arian's involvement with terrorist organizations justified his firing. "It's imperative, under the conditions of 9/11 and the interruptions on the campus, that we act," Beard said. "It's not about what he says. It's about what he's doing to this university. And he doesn't seem to care."[110] Thomas M. Gonzalez, an attorney who wrote the legal opinion used to justify the decision, said Al-Arian had repeatedly failed to identify himself as a private citizen rather than a university representative when speaking on matters of public controversy. "Dr. Al-Arian's rights under the First Amendment must be balanced against the recognized right of USF, as Dr. Al-Arian's employer, to achieve its purpose of education."[111] Judy L. Genshaft, the university's president, defended the board's decision and initiated action to dismiss Al-Arian in December 2001. "After much thought, I have come to the sad conclusion that if Dr. Al-Arian remains an employee of the University, the certainty of prolonged disruption of the University and the continuing threat to our students, faculty and staff is profoundly real," she wrote.[112]

In January 2002, Al-Arian announced his plans to appeal the board's decision. In mid-March, the American Association of University Professors sent a three-member team to USF to review the case. Professors from Duke University, Villanova University and the City University of New York met with Genshaft and Al-Arian. After the visit, Genshaft was non-committal about whether she will fire Al-Arian. "I don't have a side," she said after her meeting with the

[109]*An Ill-Fated Television Interview,* CHRON. OF HIGHER EDUC., Feb. 8, 2002, at A12.

[110]Sharon Walsh, *Blaming the Victim? A University Vows to Fire a Tenured Professor Facing Death Threats in the Wake of September 11,* CHRON. OF HIGHER EDUC., Feb. 8, 2002, at A10.

[111]The full text of Gonzalez's letter to the university's legal counsel, along with other documents in the Al-Arian case, can be found on the University of South Florida's Web site: http://www.usf.edu/news/ (visited March 30, 2002).

[112]*Id.*

visitors.[113] As of mid-May 2002, Al-Arian remained on the university's payroll, though suspended from his duties.[114] Genshaft said she intended to make a final decision in August. One of the AAUP's options is to censure the university, but a censure resolution would not come before the AAUP membership until June 2003.[115] Al-Arian's case has attracted national attention, including an editorial in the *New York Times* that denounced the USF Board of Trustees for their decision and Florida Governor Jeb Bush for supporting it. "Wartime is precisely the moment when unpopular views and the role of a university as an open forum for ideas must be most vigorously defended," the *Times* declared.[116]

DISCUSSION AND CONCLUSIONS

The reactions of the public, political leaders and university administrators to free speech on campus since 9/11 may foreshadow a disturbing breakdown in the consensus that has been the major protection of academic freedom at American colleges and universities. The degree to which academic freedom has diminished since 9/11 is a reflection of three factors: the nature and location of the terrorist attacks; the willingness of the White House, some members of Congress and others taking their lead to wrongly equate dissent with disloyalty, and the ways in which the current generation of university leaders view the role of the academy during a time of national crisis.

First, the fact that terrorists almost simultaneously hijacked four commercial airliners and caused thousands of deaths on U.S. soil caused many Americans to reassess their personal safety. The impact of these events on the American psyche cannot be measured, but it certainly was severe. No event since the Japanese attack on Pearl Harbor in 1941 has come close to the shock value of 9/11. In contrast to Pearl Harbor, Americans watched the horrific events of 9/11 unfold live on television in their own homes, schools and workplaces. Many saw the second jet hit the towers. More still watched as the

---

[113]Kathryn Wexler, *Al-Arian's Case is Weighed by Peers,* ST. PETERSBURG TIMES, Mar. 16, 2002, at 1B.

[114]Ben Feller, *Report: President Wavers on Plan to Fire Professor; Genshaft Dismisses Assessment*, TAMPA TRIBUNE, Apr. 25, 2002, at 1.

[115]*See* Brink, *supra* note 106, at 1B, and Feller, *supra* note 114, at 1. Censure would have no legal standing but might make it more difficult for USF to hire and retain faculty members. *See* Kathleen Ochsorn, *Cautionary Tale of Past USF Censure*, ST. PETERSBURG TIMES, May 5, 2002, at 1D. Ochsorn, associate professor of English and writing at the University of Tampa, reviews the AAUP's censure of the University of South Florida from 1964 to 1968 in the context of the Al-Arian case.

[116]Editorial, *Protecting Speech on Campus,* N.Y. TIMES, Jan. 27, 2002, § 4, at 12.

towers collapsed and the gruesome battle to free the living from the wreckage was fought.[117] Subsequent concern about what officials now call "homeland security" has led Congress and the executive branch to be much more willing to restrict individual liberty in the name of national security. Perhaps most importantly, many Americans have begun to question whether it is possible to be safe and secure without consenting to reductions in the level of individual freedom and liberties enjoyed in the past. Much of the debate over domestic anti-terrorism policy has been framed in terms of the assumed paradox of security versus freedom.[118]

Of the previous challenges to academic freedom in the second half of the twentieth century—McCarthyism,[119] the Vietnam War and the Persian Gulf conflict—two involved military action overseas. Only the fear of the spread of Communism that fueled McCarthyism raised some of the same concerns about an attack on America from within. The geographical proximity of the events of 9/11, the personal immediacy resulting from media coverage of the tragedy and the perceived need to prevent future attacks have combined to contribute to a climate in which Americans seem less willing to tolerate criticism of the government than at any time since the McCarthy period.

Additionally, some Republicans in Congress—particularly Senator Trent Lott and Representative Tom DeLay—have shown little tolerance for citizens or officeholders who have reservations about President Bush's policies. Their comments, along with those of Attorney General John Ashcroft, have undermined the legitimacy of those who question the objectives and tactics of the war on terrorism. Opposition to the war itself, even among religious-based peace groups, has been muted because critics fear being labeled unpatri-

[117]Among the many analyses of how Americans received and responded to news accounts of 9/11 are Lori Robertson, *Anchoring the Nation*, AM. JOURNALISM REV., Nov. 2001, at 40, and Andrew Kohut, *A Worried Public Tunes In*; *The Press Shines at a Dark Moment*, COLUM. JOURNALISM REV., Jan.–Feb. 2002, at 54.

[118]Typical of this false choice is the phrasing of a question asked by Greenberg Quinlan Rosner Research in a poll taken Dec. 4–6, 2001: "Please tell me whether you agree or disagree with the statement ' ... Americans will have to accept new restrictions on their civil liberties if we are to win the war on terrorism.'" Of 1,000 registered voters who were questioned, 35% strongly agreed with the statement and 27% somewhat agreed. Public Opinion Online, http://web.lexis-nexis.com/universe (accession number 0395765, visited March 30, 2002).

[119]While it is true that Senator Joseph McCarthy sought to expose Communists in the U.S. government, the surrender of Nationalist Forces in China to the Communist army led by Mao Zedong in mid-1949 and North Korea's attack on South Korea in June 1950 contributed to this paranoia. *See, e.g.*, RICHARD M. FREELAND, THE TRUMAN DOCTRINE AND THE ORIGINS OF MCCARTHYISM: FOREIGN POLICY, DOMESTIC POLITICS AND INTERNAL SECURITY 1946–1948 344–60 (1985).

otic. In this environment, a faculty member thinks twice before voicing a contrary or controversial opinion.

Academic freedom also has been undermined by non-academic groups having close connections to higher education. The American Council of Trustees and Alumni, a conservative group chaired by Lynne Cheney—the wife of the vice president and the former head of the National Endowment for the Humanities—issued an extensive report critical of the lack of "patriotism" of universities.[120] The report lists 115 incidents of the failure of universities to respond to 9/11 in an appropriately patriotic way. The report, which indicts universities for broadening their curricula to include Asian and Islamic studies and for not requiring students to take American history, concludes that "[i]t is urgent that students and professors who support the war against terrorism, as well as those who are opposed, not be intimidated."[121] However, the goal of ACTA seems to be to do just that; the litany of examples consists almost exclusively of anecdotal comments critical of post-9/11 U.S. policy.[122]

Perhaps the most disturbing aspect of the current climate is the failure of colleges and universities to defend the importance of academic freedom in the face of the public climate of intolerance for dissent. As the episodes detailed in this article illustrate, prominent leaders within academia have believed it necessary to publicly distance themselves from critique or to take action against campus critics of U.S. policy. These leaders include the president of the University of Texas and the chancellor of the City University of New York—two of the most prominent public universities in the country. Most of the incidents we detail do not involve direct attacks on academic freedom from entities outside academia. They do not appear to be actions that would support litigation. Most will not even lead to investigations by the AAUP. Together, however, they provide evidence of the breakdown of consensus about the importance and extent of academic freedom in the face of national crisis.

One reason may be that college and university presidents of the twenty-first century lack the historical perspective that their counterparts of thirty years ago possessed. Many of the presidents in the late 1960s and early 1970s were junior faculty members during the

[120]ACTA Report, Defending Civilization: How Are Universities Are Failing America and What Can Be Done About It (Jerry L. Martin, Anne D. Neal eds., 2002), *available at* http://www.goacta.org/reports/defciv.pdf. *See also* Jim Lobe, *The War on Dissent Widens,* AlterNet.org, http://www.alternet.org/story.html?StoryID=12612 (visited Mar. 22, 2002).

[121]*See* Defending Civilization, *supra* note 120, at 6.

[122]*Id.*

McCarthy era who would have been exposed to the negative consequences of those years on individuals and institutions. Further, these presidents likely viewed court decisions affecting academic freedom, particularly *Sweezy v. New Hampshire* and *Keyishian v. Board of Regents* through the lens of direct experience.[123] As a result, they may have had a narrower view of their own power to regulate faculty speech. Consequently, they may have been hesitant to restrict the speech of faculty members, even when under pressure from governing boards and legislators to suppress criticism of the war.[124] By contrast, today's university administrators may be less likely to have had firsthand experience with the prevailing mood of censorship that characterized McCarthyism. More importantly, they view the court's jurisprudence regarding academic freedom through the lens of history. As we pointed out, the broad language of cases like *Keyishian* has not been given substance by the Court, and the development of doctrines such as the public employee doctrine has led to a more limited view of academic freedom.

Finally, we believe that the reluctance of U.S. faculty members to engage in constructive criticism of the Bush Administration and its policies stems from a realization that their presidents are less likely to defend free speech in this climate. Even though only one professor has actually been threatened with the loss of his job, the informal mechanisms designed to promote hegemony and deter dissent are working effectively. The haste with which college presidents have sought to disavow critical or controversial statements by faculty members suggests that they, too, are cowed by the public's hostility toward contrary views. The most remarkable and troublesome aspect of the post-9/11 attacks on academic freedom is that they have weakened the continuing compact that ensured academic freedom on U.S. campuses for nearly fifty years. The failure of academic leaders—whose opinions carry weight in state capitals and Washington, D.C.—to vigorously defend their faculties' ability to speak freely on matters of public concern is one of the undocumented casualties of 9/11.

---

[123]*Keyeshian,* in particular, was viewed as a great victory for academic freedom and as the beginning of a full fledged embrace of academic freedom by the First Amendment. *See, e.g.* Byrne, *supra* note 41, at 293.

[124]Although in a slightly different context—others have made the same generational observation. *See, e.g.,* David M. Rabban, *Free Speech and Progressive Social Thought,* 74 TEX. L. REV. 951, 1035–37 (1996)(arguing that the views of today's free speech critics are tempered by their understandings of Cold War regulation of speech compared to their progressive counterparts).

7 COMM. L. & POL'Y 461–494 (2002)

COURTROOM ACCESS AFTER 9/11: A PATHOLOGICAL PERSPECTIVE

KATHLEEN K. OLSON*

The dangers that times of national stress inevitably pose for First Amendment freedoms led legal scholar Vincent Blasi to formulate what he called the "pathological perspective." Blasi argued that, because the nation is more willing to give up fundamental liberties during these periods, it is incumbent upon the courts to anticipate such times and create legal rules that will withstand such pressures. This article examines the Supreme Court's courtroom access doctrine from a pathological perspective. It concludes that the confusing legacy of the Court's decisions in courtroom access cases has increased the danger to First Amendment rights during this critical time, and it proposes a more robust doctrine of courtroom access drawn from the pathological perspective.

"Publicity is the soul of justice," legal philosopher Jeremy Bentham wrote in 1827. "Without publicity, all other checks are insufficient: in comparison of publicity, all other checks are of small account."[1] Public trials are fundamental to the American justice system, and a right of access to the courtroom is counted among the many constitutional freedoms enjoyed under the democratic system of government in the United States.

These freedoms are not immune to danger, however. In *Freedom of the Press in England 1476–1776*, Fredrick S. Siebert espoused two propositions to describe 300 years of government-press relations in England. The second proposed that "freedom contracts and the enforcement of restraints increases as the stresses on the stability of

---

*Assistant Professor, Department of Journalism and Communication, Lehigh University.

[1]JEREMY BENTHAM, RATIONALE OF JUDICIAL EVIDENCE 524 (1827), *quoted in* Richmond Newspapers, Inc. v. Virginia, 448 U.S. 555, 569 (1980).

the government and of the structure of society increase."[2] Thirty-three years after Siebert's seminal work, First Amendment scholar Vincent Blasi examined the history of the United States and found the same phenomenon at work.

Constitutional principles that are taken for granted in normal times may be challenged in times of stress, Blasi wrote, and the "core commitments" that derive from those principles may suddenly be seen as burdensome:

> In such periods, the times seem so different, so out of joint, the threats from within or without seem so unprecedented, that the Constitution itself is perceived by many persons as anachronistic, or at least rigidly, unrealistically formalistic. In times when those misgivings take hold, the central norms of the constitutional regime are in jeopardy.[3]

The pressures of such critical times and the dangers they inevitably pose for First Amendment freedoms led Blasi to formulate what he called the "pathological perspective." Blasi argued that, because the nation is more willing to give up fundamental liberties during times of great national stress, it is incumbent upon the courts to anticipate such times and create legal rules that will withstand such pressures. Courts must rule "for the worst of times," using simple principles to protect the core values of the First Amendment during periods of stress.[4]

Civil libertarians agree that the nation finds itself in the midst of pathological times.[5] The terrorist attacks of September 11, 2001, and the resulting war on terror have caused profound changes in public attitudes toward the government and civil liberties. Blasi, in describ-

---

[2]FREDRICK S. SIEBERT, FREEDOM OF THE PRESS IN ENGLAND 1476–1776: THE RISE AND DECLINE OF GOVERNMENT CONTROL 10 (1965). Siebert's First Proposition was, "The extent of government control of the press depends on the nature of the relationship of the government to those subject to the government." *Id.*

[3]Vincent Blasi, *The Pathological Perspective and the First Amendment*, 85 COLUM. L. REV. 449, 456–57 (1985).

[4]*Id.* at 449–450.

[5]*See, e.g.*, Pam Belluck, *A Nation Challenged: Civil Liberties; Hue and Murmur Over Curbed Rights,* N.Y. TIMES, Nov. 17, 2001, at B8 (describing concern of some civil libertarians about anti-terrorism measures); Robyn E. Blumner, *Bookstores and Libraries Not Safe From First Amendment Pillaging,* ST. PETERSBURG TIMES, Apr. 14, 2002, at 6D (describing as "scary" rules established by USA Patriot Act greatly increasing government's subpoena power over libraries); Carl S. Kaplan, *New Economy: Bracing for a Flood of Efforts to Control Speech as Hateful or Terrorist,* N.Y. TIMES, Feb. 11, 2002, at C3 (describing concerns of American civil libertarians over attempts to censor speech online).

ing wartime as a classic example of pathology, could be describing the dominant political climate of today:

> The stakes are high, the commitment of the political community to a specific objective is great, and even the speculative possibility that internal dissent might prevent the nation from maximizing its chances of success is troubling. If the issue is defined as a choice between national self-defense and the full realization of basic constitutional ideals, few persons would choose the latter.[6]

The USA Patriot Act,[7] passed by Congress in "furious haste"[8] by an overwhelming margin, reflects this societal unease. Among other things, the act expanded the government's ability to conduct electronic surveillance, allowed for the monitoring of attorney-client communication in some cases and greatly expanded the FBI's ability to gather domestic intelligence.[9] Blasi's concept of pathology and Siebert's Second Proposition are all too well demonstrated by the wartime panic and politics that engendered this fundamental expansion of executive power.

Congress was not the only government institution to fall prey to the pressure of pathological times. The Department of Justice and the president himself have indicated a willingness to trade fundamental constitutional principles for the chimera of security in many areas, including courtroom access.[10] The principle of open trials has been jeopardized on two fronts: in an order by the attorney general to immigration judges across the country ordering their courtrooms closed,[11] and in the proposed rules for secret mili-

---

[6]Blasi, *supra* note 3, at 464.

[7]USA Patriot Act of 2001, Pub. L. No. 107–56 (2001).

[8]Jim McGee, *An Intelligence Giant in the Making; Anti-Terrorism Law Likely to Bring Domestic Apparatus of Unprecedented Scope,* WASH. POST, Nov. 4, 2001, at A4.

[9]*Id.*

[10]*See* Elisabeth Bumiller and Katharine Q. Seelye, *Bush Defends Wartime Call for Tribunals,* N.Y. TIMES, Dec. 5, 2001, at A1 (reporting president's belief that ordinary trial procedures for suspected terrorists would compromise national security); George Lardner, Jr., *ABA Urges Ashcroft to Kill Order,* WASH. POST, Jan. 4, 2002, at A10 (describing American Bar Association's objections to attorney general's order allowing monitoring of attorney-client conversations in cases of suspected terrorism).

[11]*See* Memorandum from Michael J. Creppy, Chief Immigration Judge of the United States, to Immigration Judges and Court Administrators 1 (Sept. 21, 2001), *available at* http://news.findlaw.com/hdocs/docs/aclu/creppy092101memo.pdf [hereinafter Creppy Memorandum].

tary tribunals set forth by President George W. Bush in November 2001.[12]

Courtroom access is, of course, a constitutional issue, at least since the Supreme Court held in *Richmond Newspapers, Inc. v. Virginia*[13] in 1980 that the press and the public have a First Amendment right to attend criminal trials. This article will examine the Supreme Court's courtroom access doctrine from a pathological perspective and show that the Court shares some of the blame for recent limitations on access. By creating a confusing set of principles that gives judges too much discretion and too little guidance, the Court in *Richmond Newspapers* and its progeny increased the danger that decision makers would succumb to the pressures of the moment and restrict First Amendment rights during this critical time.

The first part of this article will review the challenges that have faced or will soon face lower court judges in ruling on the government's orders to close courtroom doors, both for immigration proceedings and for the military tribunals planned for the Guantanamo Bay detainees. The second part will discuss the pathological perspective and its usefulness in fashioning First Amendment doctrine for troubled times. Blasi's 1985 description of the insidious pressures that come to bear on the constitutional regime in pathological times bears an eerie resemblance to current events and clearly shows the need for proactive decision making regarding core constitutional values. The article will examine the current state of courtroom access doctrine, concluding that it offers little guidance to judges who must make decisions under intense political pressure. Finally, the article proposes a more robust doctrine of courtroom access, based on the pathological perspective. By both narrowing and broadening current access law, the new rule should provide the stability and clarity needed to protect the right of courtroom access, even in the worst of times.

COURTROOM ACCESS AFTER 9/11

Press organizations have already filed two lawsuits to open immigration proceedings closed by order of the attorney general,[14] and it is likely that the press would similarly protest any move to hold secret

[12]*See* Press Release, The White House, President Issues Military Order (Nov. 13, 2001), *available at* http://www.whitehouse.gov/news/releases/2001/11/pring/20011113-27.html.

[13]448 U.S. 555 (1980).

[14]Detroit News v. Ashcroft, No. 02–70340 (E.D. Mich. filed Jan. 29, 2002); North Jersey Media Group v. Ashcroft, No. 02–967 (JWB) (D.N.J. filed Mar. 6, 2002).

hearings for the detainees at Guantanamo Bay in Cuba. While the two situations differ in many respects, from the applicable legal rules[15] to the purported danger posed by openness, they share certain characteristics that mark the closures as the products of pathological times.

Administrative Proceedings: The Case of Rabih Haddad

Ten days after the terrorists' attacks in September 2001, Chief Immigration Judge Michael Creppy sent a memo to all Immigration and Naturalization Service administrative judges and court administrators stating that, due to heightened security, Attorney General John Ashcroft had ordered special procedures to be implemented for certain cases in the Immigration Court.[16] The procedures required judges "to hold the hearings individually, to close the hearing to the public, and to avoid discussing the case or otherwise disclosing any information about the case to anyone outside the Immigration Court."[17] Specific instructions further mandated that the courtroom be completely closed, with "no visitors, no family, and no press" and that precautions be taken so that absolutely no information about the case would be disclosed.[18]

On December 14, 2001, Rabih Haddad, a leader in the Muslim community of Ann Arbor, Michigan, was arrested and held by the INS on what was described as a visa violation.[19] Haddad, a native of Lebanon, was a trustee of the Global Relief Foundation, a group suspected by the U.S. government of funding terrorist activities. The offices of the foundation in Illinois had been raided the same day, and the group's assets were frozen, although no arrests were made and the group denied any link to terrorists.[20]

---

[15]The constitutional rights of the defendants in these cases, including Sixth Amendment rights, may vary depending on their status as non-citizen aliens or foreign aggressors in a time of war. For a general discussion of the due process rights afforded aliens in deportation proceedings, for example, *see* Jim Rosenfeld, *Deportation Proceedings and Due Process of Law*, 26 COLUM. HUM. RTS. L. REV. 713 (1995). Principles of courtroom access based on the First Amendment do not vary according to the status of the defendant, however, because the Court in *Richmond Newspapers* recognized a right of the public and the press to attend criminal trials that does not depend on the rights of the accused. 448 U.S. at 597–98.

[16]Creppy Memorandum, *supra* note 11, at 1.

[17]*Id.*

[18]*Id.* at 2–3.

[19]Alexandra R. Moses, *Local Community Leader Detained by INS, Groups Say*, DETROIT FREE PRESS, Dec. 17, 2001, *available at* http://www.freep.com/news/latestnews/pm6501_20011217.htm.

[20]*Id.*

Haddad was just one of more than 600 immigrants detained by the INS on immigration and criminal charges in the immediate aftermath of September 11, according to the Justice Department.[21] A closed hearing in the Haddad matter was held December 19, 2001. According to the Michigan chapter of the American Civil Liberties Union, more than 250 people were turned away from a second hearing in early January 2002.[22] At the end of January, the ACLU and its Michigan chapter filed suit in federal court to open the proceedings, naming as defendants Ashcroft, Creppy and the immigration judge assigned to Haddad's case.[23] The case was brought on behalf of two newspapers, *The Detroit News* and the *Metro Times*, and U.S. Rep. John Conyers, Jr., a Democratic congressman from Detroit and the ranking member of the House Judiciary Committee, which oversees the immigration courts and the Justice Department.

Asked Kary Moss of the Michigan chapter of the ACLU, "If hearings of this nature are being conducted in secret, how can we be sure that our justice system is really working and that detainees are being treated fairly?"[24] Under settled First Amendment law, "There is a strong presumption that court proceedings must be open to the public and members of the press," said ACLU legal director Steven Shapiro. "The Justice Department's policy of blanket secrecy is unconstitutional and incompatible with the values of a free society."[25] In April 2002, a district court judge agreed that the attorney general's blanket closure of INS proceedings was unconstitutional and granted the plaintiffs' motion to open the proceedings.[26]

---

[21]Neil A. Lewis, *Justice Dept. and Senate Clash Over Bush Actions,* N.Y. TIMES, Nov. 28, 2001, at B7.

[22]*ACLU Demands Open Court Proceedings on Immigration Case,* CIVIL LIBERTIES NEWSLETTER, February 2002, at 4, *available at* http://www.aclumich.org/nletter/february.pdf. The ACLU claimed that security personnel kept the crowd several hundred feet from the entrance of the building in which the hearing was held. *Id.*

[23]Detroit News v. Ashcroft, No. 02–70340 (E.D. Mich. filed Jan. 29, 2002).

[24]Press Release, ACLU, ACLU Files First Post-Sept. 11 Challenge to Closed Immigration Hearings on Behalf of MI Congressman and Journalists (Jan. 29, 2002), *available at* http://www.aclu.org/news/2002/n012902a.html.

[25]*Id.*

[26]Detroit Free Press v. Ashcroft,195 F. Supp. 2d 937 (E.D. Mich. 2002). A similar lawsuit was filed in early March 2002 challenging the constitutionality of closed immigration hearings in New Jersey. The suit was filed on behalf of *The New Jersey Law Journal* and the West Paterson *Herald News*. *See* North Jersey Media Group v. Ashcroft, No. 02–967 (JWB) (D.N.J. filed March 6, 2002). *See also Civil Liberties Groups Sue U.S. on Closed Immigration Hearings,* N.Y. TIMES, Mar. 7, 2002, at B7.

Secret Military Tribunals

On November 13, 2001, President Bush issued a military order authorizing a military commission to try non-U.S. citizens suspected of being members of al-Qaeda or of having "engaged in, aided or abetted, or conspired to commit, acts of international terrorism, or acts in preparation therefore."[27] These proposed military tribunals would be directed under the "exclusive jurisdiction" of the Secretary of Defense. The order stated that judicial review of the proceedings would not be allowed and that general legal principles governing criminal trials may be suspended: "Given the danger to the safety of the United States and the nature of international terrorism, ... it is not practicable to apply the principles of law ... generally recognized in the trial of criminal cases in the United States district courts."[28]

Bush's order sparked immediate protest from groups as varied as the ACLU and the Cato Institute,[29] as well as negative editorials[30] and commentary in the press.[31] The American Bar Association registered its concern that defendants tried before the tribunals would not be afforded basic protections, such as the presumption of innocence, and decried the possibility that the trials may be held in secret.[32]

Bush defended the order as the result of "extraordinary times,"[33] but the outcry caused the administration to rewrite many of the rules to more closely resemble those of criminal trials. The tribunals would be "largely open to the public" after all, officials said, except

---

[27]Press Release, White House, President Issues Military Order (Nov. 13, 2001), *available at* http://www.whitehouse.gov/news/releases/2001/11/print/20011113-27.html.

[28]*Id.*

[29]*See, e.g.,* William Glaberson, *Groups Gird for Long Legal Fight on New Bush Anti-Terror Powers,* N.Y. TIMES, Nov. 30, 2001, at A1; Robert A. Levy, *Don't Shred the Constitution to Fight Terror,* WALL ST. J., Nov. 20, 2001, at A18.

[30]*See, e.g., Secrecy Taints Bush Plan for Trying Suspected Terrorists,* USA TODAY, Nov. 16, 2001, at 14A; *Don't Shortcut Justice,* S. F. CHRON., Nov. 15, 2001, at A28.

[31]*See, e.g.,* Diane Carman, *Military Trial Not Path to Justice,* DENVER POST, Nov. 15, 2001, at B-01; William Safire, *Seizing Dictatorial Power,* N.Y. TIMES, Nov. 15, 2001, at A31. Not all the commentary was negative, however. *See, e.g.,* Douglas W. Kmiec, *Tribunals are Necessary in Times of War,* WALL ST. J., Nov. 15, 2001, at A26; Jerome M. Marcus, *Military Tribunals Protect Intelligence, Provide Justice,* ST. LOUIS POST-DISPATCH, Nov. 18, 2001, at B3.

[32]*Bar Association Asks for Legal Safeguards at Military Tribunals; White House Had Wanted Group to Refrain from Taking a Position,* ST. LOUIS POST-DISPATCH, Feb. 5, 2002, at A5.

[33]James Gerstenzang, *Bush Defends Trying Terror Suspects in Secret Military Tribunals,* L.A. TIMES, Nov. 20, 2001, at A3.

for portions that would be closed for national security reasons.[34] Concerns remained despite the reassurances and the proposed changes,[35] however, and knowledgeable sources said the location of the tribunals at Guantanamo Bay would make access difficult because the site would be strictly controlled by the U.S. military.[36]

Important constitutional principles are at stake in the closure of the INS proceedings in Michigan and New Jersey, as well as in potential rulings on access to the Guantanamo Bay tribunals. Unfortunately, the judges in these proceedings must make critical decisions in a time of great political pressure, and a natural tendency is to opt for security over freedom.

"We are at the 'Korematsu' crossroads," Harvard law professor Laurence Tribe warned the Senate Judiciary Committee in hearings about the proposed military order. "[T]he war on terrorism does not require us to sacrifice constitutional principles on the altar of public safety."[37] Experience has shown, however, that in times of national stress, fundamental rights have sometimes been sacrificed in the name of security or other perceived national interests.[38] Such times are what Blasi calls pathological periods, the subject of the next section.

THE PATHOLOGICAL PERSPECTIVE

According to legal scholar Vincent Blasi, difficult times require a strong commitment to First Amendment values,[39] but during pathological times, events conspire to weaken the resolve of both the public and the judiciary and the commitment to those values.

---

[34]John Mintz, *Extended Detention in Cuba Mulled; Officials Indicate Guantanamo Bay Could Hold Tribunals, Carry Out Sentences*, WASH. POST, Feb. 13, 2002, at A16.

[35]*See, e.g.*, Press Release, ACLU, ACLU Troubled by Reports that Potentially Secret Military Tribunals Could Place Life or Death of Defendant Solely in Hands of President (Mar. 20, 2002), *available at* http://www.aclu.org/news/2002/n032002c.html.

[36]Mintz, *supra* note 34, at 16.

[37]*Department of Justice Oversight: Preserving Our Freedoms While Defending Against Terrorism: Hearing Before the Senate Comm. on the Judiciary*, 107th Cong. (2001) (statement of Laurence H. Tribe, Tyler Professor of Constitutional Law, Harvard Law School), *available at* http://judiciary.senate.gov/testimony.cfm?id=129&wit_id=73, *citing* Korematsu *v.* United States, 323 U.S. 214 (1944) (upholding World War II Japanese internment camps).

[38]*See, e.g.*, Dennis v. United States, 341 U.S. 494 (1951) (McCarthyism); Hirabayashi v. United States, 320 U.S. 81 (1943) (World War II Japanese relocation camps); Schenck v. United States, 249 U.S. 47 (1919) (the "Red Scare").

[39]Blasi, *supra* note 3, at 450.

Because it is less likely that the legislature or even the judiciary will act to further First Amendment values in the face of national security or other pressures, Blasi contended that courts should act *ex ante* to protect core First Amendment values from diminution. Pathological periods are marked by a shift in the tolerance afforded unorthodox views and by a shift in fundamental attitudes among those "whose judgments have an important influence on the general level and vigor of public debate and private inquiry."[40] This attitude shift may manifest itself at the legislative or executive levels of government or may cause judges to interpret the First Amendment more restrictively than they normally would. A period is pathological, Blasi wrote, "when social or political conditions in the relevant community (national, regional, or local) generate a shift in attitudes regarding toleration that places in jeopardy one or more of the commitments that comprise the core of the First Amendment."[41]

In order to preserve core First Amendment values, courts should adopt the "pathological perspective" during ordinary times and formulate doctrine with an emphasis on how well it would serve during times of stress. First Amendment doctrine, he wrote, "should be targeted for the worst of times."[42]

The proposition was not completely new. In *Dennis v. United States*, Justice Felix Frankfurter warned against allowing "the impregnating atmosphere of the times" to compromise impartiality when making rulings on controversial matters. Instead, he said, constitutional issues "must be determined by principles established in cases decided in more tranquil periods."[43]

The pathological perspective is based on several key assertions. First, for constitutional authority to be respected as superior, including by those who exercise political power, a constitutional tradition must be built on a limited number of relatively stable central norms.[44] To Blasi, certain norms of free expression and inquiry—freedom of association, unrestricted use of public forums, freedom from governmental monitoring, among others[45]—represent

---

[40]*Id.*

[41]*Id.* at 466.

[42]*Id.* at 450.

[43]341 U.S. 494, 528 (1951) (Frankfurter, J., concurring) (upholding convictions of Communists under the Smith Act).

[44]Blasi, *supra* note 3, at 455. That is not to say that constitutional norms are static. Blasi admits that adaptation and "creative innovation" are important at the margins, but holds that this view does not undermine the importance of a "core of relatively stable and consistently enforced central norms." *Id.* at 454–55.

[45]*Id.* at 460–61.

core values of the American constitutional tradition and must therefore be preserved and strengthened whenever possible. Because he viewed the essential nature of constitutional government as preservative, his thesis is a limited one. The aim of the pathological perspective, he argued, is to maintain "the theoretical integrity and practical effectiveness of a limited number of propositions that can be said to constitute the 'core' of the speech, press, and assembly clauses" of the First Amendment.[46]

Why can't normal constitutional adjudication fashion a system strong enough to withstand challenge during pathological times? Blasi argued that the everyday legal maneuvering and shaping of legal arguments that is normal and appropriate in the American adversary system serves to undercut the authority of constitutional norms:

> When [central constitutional] norms are not themselves under challenge, their main function is to serve as starting points for analogy or argumentation in disputes over the outer reaches of constitutional doctrine. ... The grist of everyday legal argumentation is the manipulation of ideas. That tradition of manipulation, though perfectly appropriate in adversarial discourse, may make it more difficult for the central norms of the constitutional regime to carry the authority they must—to evoke the reverence and deep conviction they must—if those norms are to withstand pathological pressures.[47]

The pathological perspective does not require fundamental changes in constitutional principles. Rather, a court adopting the pathological perspective would change its priority to the preservation and strengthening of those central norms that lie at the core of the constitutional regime and that are most likely to be challenged during times of national stress. The pathological perspective would affect both the way judges reason about free speech issues and the specific principles and outcomes of particular cases. Rather than relying on complex legal tests, judges (and therefore lawyers) would analyze issues with an eye to core values and traditional commitments. Where precedent cannot guide the court, simplicity can: Under the pathological perspective, judicial decisions should make sense to those with an unsophisticated understanding of the law. Blasi wrote:

---

[46]*Id.* at 452.
[47]*Id.* at 458–59.

> Both because judicial authority is threatened in times of stress and because the most important phenomenon during such periods is a shift in attitudes, a judicial heritage targeted for the worst of times must speak to persons who are neither First Amendment specialists nor devotees. The heritage must speak, moreover, in confident tones that do not invite critical reflection and doubt regarding the importance of free speech.[48]

Blasi lamented that First Amendment doctrine lacks the simplicity of analysis that the pathological perspective requires, although he offered no solutions. Simplicity of analysis should be coupled, according to Blasi, with what might be labeled "clarity of description." In order to avert the shift in attitudes that is the danger during pathological periods, the ability to frame a principle in terms of a simple precept can be effective. "Under the First Amendment there is no such thing as a false idea" or "The best test of truth is the power of the thought to get itself accepted in the competition of the market"—these "well-worn homilies" have emotional force and can play a valuable role in averting intolerance.[49]

Homilies are not enough, however. What is needed is what Blasi calls a "middle ground" between reliance on simple precepts and reliance on "the enervating contingencies and complexities of contemporary First Amendment doctrine."[50] The answer is a return to principles—"value proposition[s] of sufficient generality and thrust that for a fair number of particular cases acceptance or rejection of the proposition constitutes a major variable in determining how a case is resolved."[51]

Principles such as the prohibition against prior restraints have "thrust":[52] Unlike multi-factor balancing tests or context-dependent standards, their adoption represents a value commitment that strongly directs how a particular dispute will be adjudicated.[53] Still, a First Amendment principle need not be absolute; countervailing considerations may outweigh its initial thrust, and definitional problems will always remain. But the process of defining a First Amendment principle requires that concepts be clarified and decisions about compatibility and priority be made.

---

[48]*Id.* at 471.

[49]*Id.* at 472, *quoting* Abrams v. United States, 250 U.S. 616, 630 (1919) (Holmes, J., dissenting) and Gertz v. Robert Welch, Inc., 418 U.S. 323, 339 (1974).

[50]*Id.*

[51]*Id.* at 473.

[52]*Id.*

[53]*Id.*

For judges trying to make the right decision during times of extreme pressure,

> a mode of analysis that emphasizes principles ... can broaden the perspective of the decisionmaker and make the regulatory concerns of the moment seem less monumental. ... A legal culture that talks and thinks in terms of principles is somewhat less likely, by virtue of that mode of discourse, to trivialize its ideals in the process of case-by-case application, or lose the capacity to subject its *ad hoc*, pragmatic impulses to some form of discipline.[54]

Furthermore, because stability and clarity are so important, "in crafting standards to govern specific areas of First Amendment dispute, courts that adopt the pathological perspective should place a premium on confining the range of discretion left to future decisionmakers who will be called upon to make judgments when pathological pressures are most intense."[55]

Blasi did not assert that the pathological perspective would always prevent the destructive social dynamics that occur during times of national stress. "The most we can hope for," he said, "is that well-prepared methodologies and doctrines might help to blunt or delay the impact of some pathological pressures, keep a pathology in certain bounds, or stimulate the regenerative forces that permit a political community to work its way out of a pathological period." This, he concluded, should not be undervalued, because the long-run consequences of pathological times can be substantial. The Red Scare of the 1910s, the McCarthy era and even the Hollywood Blacklist caused significant changes in our foreign policy and political and social life. "Pathological periods tend to be short-lived," Blasi said, "but their consequences linger on."[56]

THE EXISTING LAW OF COURTROOM ACCESS

If First Amendment doctrine shaped by the pathological perspective can prevent constitutional crises during times of national stress by protecting core values, how well does the current law on courtroom access serve that purpose? Viewed from the pathological perspective, courtroom access is a failure. Instead of stability and

---

[54] *Id.*
[55] *Id.*
[56] *Id.* at 457–58.

clarity, the Supreme Court's jurisprudence on courtroom access is marked by contradiction and confusion.

Legal scholars have noted the difficulty with which the Court has struggled with the issue of courtroom access and have criticized "the fundamental inconsistency"[57] of the Court's decisions in the two major cases that deal with the issue, *Gannett v. DePasquale*[58] and *Richmond Newspapers, Inc. v. Virginia*.[59] Even after the Court made clear in *Richmond Newspapers* that a First Amendment-based right of access exists, the parameters of that right remained unclear. Legal scholars engaged in complicated analyses in their attempts to analogize the Court's rulings to new types of proceedings,[60] and trial judges were just as confused.[61] How far the Court intended a right of access to extend continues to be a source of disagreement among lower courts.[62]

The convoluted jurisprudence of courtroom access doctrine is somewhat surprising given the long and storied history of open trials. Public trials date to the nation's founding[63] and have roots in the earliest English common law before that.[64] In 1948, Justice Hugo Black wrote, "It is 'the law of the land' that no man's life, liberty or property be forfeited as a punishment until there has been a charge

---

[57]Lewis F. Weakland, *Confusion in the Courthouse: The Legacy of the Gannett and Richmond Newspapers Public Right of Access Cases*, 59 S. CAL. L. REV. 603, 603 (1986).

[58]443 U.S. 368 (1979).

[59]448 U.S. 555 (1980).

[60]*See, e.g.*, Beth Hornbuckle Fleming, *First Amendment Right of Access to Pretrial Proceedings in Criminal Cases*, 32 EMORY L.J. 619 (1983) (concluding that an application of the Court's analysis requires a recognition of a First Amendment right of access to all pretrial proceedings, with the possible exception of grand jury proceedings); Jeanne L. Nowaczewski, *The First Amendment Right of Access to Civil Trials After Globe Newspaper Co. v. Superior Court*, 51 U. CHI. L. REV. 286 (1984) (using the historical and structural analysis of the Court to extrapolate a constitutional right of access to civil trials).

[61]*Compare* Publicker Indus. v. Cohen, 733 F.2d 1059 (3d. Cir. 1984) (reversing district court's decision to motions hearings in civil litigation) *with* San Bernardino Co. Dept. of Pub. Social Services v. Superior Court, 232 Cal. App. 3d 188 (Cal. Ct. App. 1991) (directing juvenile court to vacate its order allowing press access to juvenile dependency proceedings).

[62]*See generally* 39 A.L.R.5th 103 (1996) (listing cases); Matthew D. Bunker, JUSTICE AND THE MEDIA: RECONCILING FAIR TRIALS AND A FREE PRESS 101–115 (1997). *See also* cases cited at *infra* notes 138–45 and accompanying text.

[63]A criminal defendant's right to a public trial predated the Constitution in the United States, appearing in state constitutions as early as 1776. *See, e.g.*, Pennsylvania Declaration of Rights, 1776, IX; and North Carolina Declaration of Rights, 1776, IX, *cited in* Richmond Newspapers, Inc. v. Virginia, 448 U.S. 555, 590 (1980).

[64]*See* In re Oliver, 333 U.S. 257, 266 n.14 (1948) (citing commentators who have noted the tradition dating from as early as 1565).

fairly made and fairly tried in a public tribunal."[65] Indeed, the text of the Sixth Amendment guarantees a criminal defendant the right to a "public trial."[66]

At the same time, however, the Sixth Amendment guarantees the defendant an impartial jury.[67] Public trials can endanger this right if prejudicial publicity improperly influences jury members. Trial judges, therefore, have been forced to find ways to balance the defendant's Sixth Amendment rights with the media's First Amendment right to report on trials.[68] One method, the imposition of gag orders on the press, was severely restricted by the Court's 1976 decision in *Nebraska Press Association v. Stuart*[69] that such orders constituted unconstitutional prior restraint. Trial judges were thus forced to try other methods of protecting defendants' rights to fair trials. Rather than limit what information the press could print, therefore, trial judges began to limit what information the press could gather by closing courtrooms.

The idea that the First Amendment gives the public and the press a right of access to the courtroom, independent of the rights of the defendant, is relatively recent. The Court's decision in *Richmond Newspapers*, recognizing a First Amendment right of the public and the press to attend criminal trials, was a historic decision that significantly expanded constitutional protection to newsgathering. That it was so far-reaching was all the more surprising, coming on the heels of a case in which the Court restricted courtroom access through a narrow reading of the Sixth Amendment. The facts in *Gannett v. DePasquale*[70] centered on a pretrial suppression hearing, but the Court's analysis was not limited to the pretrial activities. The Court's ruling, upholding the closure of a pretrial proceeding based on the Sixth Amendment's public trial provision, signaled that courtroom closures would be tolerated by the Court.[71]

---

[65]*Id.* at 278.

[66]The Sixth Amendment reads, "In all criminal prosecutions, the accused shall enjoy the right to a speedy and public trial, by an impartial jury … ." U.S. CONST. amend. VI. The right exists at both the federal and state court levels, of course, because the Bill of Rights is applicable to the states through the Fourteenth Amendment. *See* Duncan v. Louisiana, 391 U.S. 145 (1968) (Sixth Amendment is applicable to states). *See also* Near v. Minnesota, 283 U.S. 697 (1931) (First Amendment is applicable to states).

[67]U.S. CONST. amend. VI.

[68]*See* Sheppard v. Maxwell, 384 U.S. 333, 357–363 (1966) (giving list of suggested ways to protect defendant's right to a fair trial).

[69]427 U.S. 539 (1976).

[70]443 U.S. 368 (1979).

[71]*Id.* at 379–84.

Gannett was the first in a series of fractured Supreme Court cases in which the justices disagreed on the scope, timing, constitutional source and purpose of a right of public access to trials. Justice Potter Stewart wrote the majority opinion, although three of the justices who joined him also wrote separate opinions.[72] "The Constitution nowhere mentions any right of access to a criminal trial on the part of the public," he wrote. "Its guarantee, like the others enumerated, is personal to the accused."[73]

While Stewart admitted to "a common law rule of open civil and criminal proceedings"[74] and "strong societal interests in public trials,"[75] he held that public access did not rise to the level of a constitutional right. Pretrial proceedings, in particular, had traditionally been closed, and the trial judge in this case was correct in finding that an open proceeding would "pose a reasonable probability of prejudice" to the defendants that mandated closure.[76] The Court concluded that "members of the public have no constitutional right under the Sixth and Fourteenth Amendments to attend criminal trials."[77]

Stewart deflected the issue of whether the First and Fourteenth Amendments gave the public a right of access by stating that, assuming *arguendo* that such a right existed, the trial judge had taken it into account but had decided any such right was outweighed by the defendant's right to a fair trial.[78] The *Gannett* decision was met with a chorus of disapproval from journalists and legal commentators alike, with Gannett chairman Allen Neuharth calling it "Star Chamber justice."[79]

Trial judges were quick to take advantage of the Court's ruling, however. Within a week of the Court's decision, a Maryland court closed a pretrial hearing based on *Gannett*[80] and the Virginia Supreme Court relied on it in upholding the closing of a criminal trial in

---

[72]Chief Justice Warren Burger and Justices Lewis Powell, William Rehnquist and John Paul Stevens joined Stewart's opinion; all but Stevens wrote separate opinions. *See id.* at 394 (Burger, C.J., concurring), *id.* at 397 (Powell, J., concurring), *id.* at 403 (Rehnquist, J., concurring).

[73]443 U.S. at 379–80.

[74]*Id.* at 384.

[75]*Id.* at 383.

[76]*Id.* at 392–93.

[77]*Id.* at 391.

[78]*Id.* at 393.

[79]*Slamming the Courtroom Doors,* TIME, July 16, 1979, at 66. *See also* James Russell Wiggins, *Mistreating Cooley's Treatise*, WASH. POST, Dec. 7, 1979, at A17 (criticizing constitutional basis of Court's ruling).

[80]Saundra Saperstein, *Judge Shuts Maryland Pretrial Hearing; Controversial Supreme Court Ruling Invoked*, WASH. POST, July 19, 1979, at A1.

the case that would become *Richmond Newspapers*.[81] The Reporters Committee for Freedom of the Press counted more than a hundred cases of closed courtrooms in the year after *Gannett*.[82]

Richmond Newspapers, Inc. v. Virginia

One year to the day after the *Gannett* decision, the Supreme Court found a First Amendment right of public access to the courts in *Richmond Newspapers*. The case was hailed as a victory for the press and seen as an important constitutional development.[83] For the first time, the Court had recognized a First Amendment right of access to governmental information, something it had been unwilling to do in earlier cases involving prison access.[84] Justice Stevens' concurring opinion described the Court as holding "unequivocally ... that an arbitrary interference with access to important information is an abridgement of the freedoms of speech and of the press."[85]

At issue in the case was the third retrial of a defendant accused of murdering a hotel manager in Virginia. The judge, acting under the authority of state law, closed the courtroom to the public. The excluded newspapers appealed the closing to the Virginia Supreme Court, which denied their petition,[86] and the case reached the Supreme Court.

In a plurality opinion, Chief Justice Warren Burger distinguished *Gannett* as having involved a pretrial proceeding and the defendant's, rather than the public's, rights. The question in *Richmond Newspapers*, he wrote, was "whether a criminal trial itself may be closed to the public upon the unopposed request of a defendant, without any demonstration that closure is required to protect the defendant's [Sixth Amendment] right to a fair trial, or that some other overriding consideration requires closure."[87] The Court said no,

---

[81]Eugene Cerruti, *"Dancing in the Courthouse": The First Amendment Right of Access Opens a New Round*, 29 U. RICH. L. REV. 237, 262 (1995).

[82]WAYNE OVERBECK, MAJOR PRINCIPLES OF MEDIA LAW 296 (2002).

[83]*See, e.g.*, Lillian R. BeVier, *Like Mackerel in the Moonlight: Some Reflections on Richmond Newspapers*, 10 HOFSTRA L. REV. 311 (1982) (case "may well signal the arrival of an expansive new First Amendment doctrine"); Anthony Lewis, *A Right to Be Informed*, N.Y. TIMES, July 3, 1980, at A19. Indeed, Justice Stevens called it a "watershed case," 448 U.S. 555, 582 (Stevens, J., concurring).

[84]*See, e.g.*, Saxbe v. Washington Post Co., 417 U.S. 843 (1974) (no constitutional right of access to federal prisons); Pell v. Procunier, 417 U.S. 817 (1974) (no constitutional right of access to state prisons).

[85]448 U.S. 555, 583 (1980) (Stevens, J., concurring).

[86]*Id.* at 562.

[87]*Id.* at 563–64.

holding that the First Amendment required that criminal trials be open to the public absent an overriding interest articulated in findings by the court.[88]

Despite its watershed status, the Court in *Richmond Newspapers* was too divided to establish a clear-cut doctrine of courtroom access. With seven separate opinions, the case was "a cacophony of judicial voices"[89] that left the newly derived right of access with no clear definition.

The two principal opinions in the case were Burger's plurality and William J. Brennan's concurrence.[90] Both justices adopted a two-pronged analysis that used history and a functional or structural model to find a First Amendment right of access to criminal trials. Their emphases were different, however, with Burger relying more heavily on a historical analysis that served ultimately to limit the scope of the right and treat the question as a narrow one.

"The historical evidence," Burger wrote, "demonstrates conclusively that at the time when our organic laws were adopted, criminal trials both here and in England had long been presumptively open."[91] His opinion traced the history of the criminal trial from before the Norman Conquest in England and concluded that, "throughout its evolution, the trial has been open to all who cared to observe."[92]

Public trials have traditionally had "therapeutic value" as well, he wrote.[93] Open trials provide "an outlet for community concern, hostility, and emotion,"[94] as well as education about the justice system that leads to confidence in its operation.[95] And public oversight of trials helps ensure that fairness prevails, by discouraging misbehavior on the part of parties and witnesses and abuse of power by judges and prosecutors.[96]

To Burger, history was important both in understanding the tradition upon which the Constitution was built and for determining its functional role. The tradition of access was no historical quirk,

---

[88]*Id.* at 581.

[89]BeVier, *supra* note 83, at 313. Justice Rehnquist was the lone dissenter, but there were six other opinions. Justice Powell did not participate in the case.

[90]Justices White and Stevens joined Burger; Justice Marshall joined Brennan.

[91]448 U.S. at 569.

[92]*Id.* at 564–65.

[93]*Id.* at 569.

[94]*Id.* at 571.

[95]*Id.* at 572.

[96]*Id.* at 569.

but was "an indispensable attribute of an Anglo-American trial,"[97] he wrote.

A common law tradition of openness, however, would not be sufficient standing alone. Rather, courtroom access should receive constitutional protection because its function was to facilitate the exercise of those rights the First Amendment was adopted to protect:

> The Bill of Rights was enacted against the backdrop of the long history of trials being presumptively open. Public access to trials was then regarded as an important aspect of the process itself. ... In guaranteeing freedoms such as those of speech and press, the First Amendment can be read as protecting the right of everyone to attend trials so as to give meaning to those explicit guarantees.[98]

Without the freedom to attend criminal trials, a freedom enjoyed for centuries, "important aspects of freedom of speech and 'of the press could be eviscerated.'"[99]

Burger's argument also linked the First Amendment right of assembly to the case, making what might be considered a public forum argument for courtroom access.[100] "A trial courtroom is also a public place where the people generally—and representatives of the media—have a right to be present," he wrote, "and where their presence historically has been thought to enhance the integrity and quality of what takes place."[101]

To Burger, all of these factors justified a finding that the right to attend criminal trials is implicit in the guarantees of the First Amendment. His opinion concluded, therefore, that, "absent an overriding interest articulated in findings [by the judge], the trial of a criminal case must be open to the public."[102]

In his concurrence, Brennan agreed that history was important to the analysis, both because the Constitution bears the "gloss" of history and because "the case for a right of access has special force when drawn from an enduring and vital tradition of public entree to particular proceedings or information."[103] Furthermore, a tradition of openness shows that access has gained the "favorable judgment of

---

[97]*Id.*
[98]*Id.* at 575.
[99]*Id.* at 580, *quoting* Branzburg v. Hayes, 408 U.S. 665, 681 (1972).
[100]*Id.* at 577–78.
[101]*Id.* at 578.
[102]*Id.* at 581.
[103]*Id.* at 589 (Brennan, J., concurring).

experience."[104] Brennan also echoed the functional purposes of courtroom access that Burger had listed[105] and its importance in furthering First Amendment values and assuring the fair operation of the judicial system.

But Brennan went further in his analysis of the functional role of open trials, based on his belief in a structural model of the First Amendment. His model holds that the First Amendment is not only a commitment to free expression for its own sake, but because it "has a *structural* role to play in securing and fostering our republican system of self-government."[106]

Brennan's structuralism was rooted in the self-governance theory of legal philosopher Alexander Meiklejohn. Meiklejohn believed that a citizen serves as "sovereign master" over the public servants who make up the government. A sovereign citizen must have access to information about important governmental issues.[107]

In an address at the dedication of the S.I. Newhouse Center for Law and Justice shortly after the *Gannett* decision, Brennan outlined his structural model and contrasted it with what he called the traditional "speech model" of the Court. While the speech model prohibited interference with freedom of expression, it did not go beyond that. His structural model, in contrast, allowed for affirmative rights under the First Amendment in order to "protect the structure of communication necessary for the existence of our democracy."[108] As an example, Brennan suggested that the press's role in "providing and circulating the information necessary for informed public discussion" should receive unique First Amendment protection.[109]

Implicit in the structural model is the necessity for debate on public issues that is not only "uninhibited, robust, and wide-open," but informed.[110] Thus, the press should be shielded not only when it speaks out, but when it performs any of the tasks necessary to gather

---

[104]*Id.* (Brennan, J., concurring).

[105]Id. at 592, 595–96 (Brennan, J., concurring)

[106]*Id.* at 586–97 (Brennan, J., concurring) (emphasis in original).

[107]*See generally* ALEXANDER MEIKLEJOHN, POLITICAL FREEDOM: THE CONSTITUTIONAL POWERS OF THE PEOPLE 55 (1960). Thomas Emerson also saw room for a right to know within his "system of free expression." The right to receive communications and the right to obtain information as a basis for transmitting ideas or facts to others constituted "the reverse side of the right to communicate" and were "inseparable and equally valued." *See* Thomas I. Emerson, *Legal Foundations of the Right to Know,* 1976 WASH. U. L.Q. 1, 2.

[108]*Address by William J. Brennan, Jr.*, 32 RUTGERS L. REV. 173, 176 (1979).

[109]*Id.* at 177.

[110]*Richmond Newspapers,* 448 U.S. at 587 (Brennan, J., concurring), *quoting* New York Times Co. v. Sullivan, 376 U.S. 254, 270 (1964).

or disseminate the news. Because the judicial system is "a coordinate branch of the *government*,"[111] information about its workings is critical for the proper functioning of our democracy, and, therefore, "trial access possesses specific structural significance."[112]

Brennan was aware that his structural model could be read to expand the public's right to know to any government-related information,[113] or indeed, beyond governmental affairs to include business-related information or any other type of information a free society may require for informed public discussion. Because the extent of First Amendment protection under his model was "theoretically endless,"[114] he wrote, the right to gather information in a particular case must be weighed against countervailing interests with the guidance of two "helpful principles": an examination of the tradition of openness for the particular proceeding and an assessment of the "specific structural value" of public access in the circumstances.[115]

In the context of trials, then, a court "must weigh the importance of public access to the trial process itself."[116] Because criminal trials have historically been open and, more significantly for Brennan, because of "the importance of public access to the broader purposes of the trial process" within the system of self-government, the Virginia statute authorizing closure of the courtroom at the sole discretion of the judge violated the First Amendment.[117]

Thus, the two principal opinions in *Richmond Newspapers* had much in common. Burger and Brennan agreed that the instrumental purposes inherent in public trials were of sufficient value to weigh in favor of the constitutional right and that history was important.

Where the two justices differed was in what mattered most. To Burger, it was history: Trials must be public because they have always been so, and this imbues them with a unique quality as an inherently public event. To Brennan, the primary value of a public trial

[111]*Id.* at 595 (Brennan, J., concurring) (emphasis in original).

[112]*Id.* at 593–94 (Brennan, J., concurring).

[113]Indeed, such a right has been expounded by legal commentators over the years, although it has not been adopted in any general way by the Court. *See, e.g.*, Thomas I. Emerson, *Legal Foundations of the Right to Know*, 1976 WASH. U. L.Q. 1; James C. Goodale, *Legal Pitfalls in the Right to Know*, 1976 WASH. U. L.Q. 29; Thomas C. Hennings, Jr., *Constitutional Law: The People's Right to Know*, 45 A.B.A. J. 667 (1959); Eric G. Olsen, Note, *The Right to Know in First Amendment Analysis*, 57 TEX. L. REV. 505 (1979).

[114]*Richmond Newspapers*, 448 U.S. at 588 (Brennan, J., concurring), *quoting* Brennan, *supra* note 108, at 177.

[115]*Id.* at 589, 598 (Brennan, J., concurring).

[116]*Id.* at 589 (Brennan, J., concurring).

[117]*Id.* at 598 (Brennan, J., concurring).

lay in its place in the constitutional framework, and the historical evidence served to confirm the importance of that role. Brennan's structuralism differs from Burger's more functional view of the value of public trials in its level of utility. To Burger, courtroom access was important because it directly furthers justice itself, through education, oversight and catharsis.[118] These instrumental values may be subordinate to other, more important values, such as the defendant's right to a fair trial or national security. While Brennan agreed that countervailing interests may outweigh the right of access, his threshold for that to occur was much higher than Burger's. These differences in their analyses would put the two justices at odds in the Court's next courtroom access case.

Globe Newspaper Co. v. Superior Court

Neither Burger nor Brennan saw the First Amendment right of access to the courtroom as absolute; closure may be justified to protect countervailing interests. Key to the Court's ruling in *Richmond Newspapers* was that the Virginia statute gave unfettered discretion to a trial judge to close a courtroom, as long as the closure itself would not impair the defendant's right to a fair trial.[119]

The standard for judging the importance of the countervailing interests was not given much attention by the Court in *Richmond Newspapers*. The Court required that a trial judge release findings that articulate "an overriding interest" in closing the trial.[120] Brennan stated that, while an examination of countervailing interests must be made, the blanket nature of the statute made unnecessary a finding of what interests might be "sufficiently compelling" to weigh against access.[121]

The Court articulated the standard for closure in *Globe Newspaper Co. v. Superior Court*,[122] a 1982 case that marked another shift in the Court's thinking about courtroom access. In *Globe*, Brennan's structural analysis was adopted by a majority of the Court, and the historical prong was relegated to secondary status.

At issue was a Massachusetts statute that mandated closure of trials during a minor's testimony in a rape trial. On appeal of a closure order, the Massachusetts Supreme Judicial Court followed the

[118] *Id.* at 569–73.
[119] *Id.* at 560 n.2.
[120] *Id.* at 581.
[121] *Id.* at 598 (Brennan, J., concurring).
[122] 457 U.S. 596 (1982).

reasoning of Burger's plurality opinion in *Richmond Newspapers* and found history controlling. Because there was no historical tradition of openness in sexual offense trials in Massachusetts, the court found the closure order constitutional and dismissed the newspaper's appeal.[123]

The Supreme Court reversed, finding that the mandatory closure statute violated the public's First Amendment right of access to criminal trials. Although Brennan and Burger both applied the two-pronged test from *Richmond Newspapers*, their analyses and ultimate outcomes were strikingly different. This time, Brennan spoke for the Court, while Burger wrote in dissent.

Brennan's opinion, joined by Justices Byron White, Thurgood Marshall, Harry Blackmun and Lewis Powell, was based squarely on his structural model. The First Amendment protects a right of access to criminal trials, Brennan wrote, both because of a long tradition of openness and because the right of access "plays a particularly significant role in the functioning of the judicial process and the government as a whole."[124]

While Brennan affirmed the value of an inquiry into historical tradition, it did not figure into his analysis. The state had applied the historical test from *Richmond Newspapers* and found no tradition of openness for rape trials. To Brennan, however, this was irrelevant:

> In *Richmond Newspapers,* the Court discerned a First Amendment right of access to *criminal trials* based in part on the recognition that as a general matter criminal trials have long been presumptively open. Whether the First Amendment right of access to criminal trials can be restricted in the context of any particular criminal trial, such as a murder trial (the setting for the dispute in *Richmond Newspapers*) or a rape trial, depends not on the historical openness of that type of criminal trial but rather on the state interests assertedly supporting the restriction.[125]

Thus, because a general right of access to criminal trials had already been established, Brennan seemed to say, the particular *type* of criminal trial did not matter.

Burger disagreed. His dissent, joined by Justice William Rehnquist, was a strongly worded defense of the history prong and its importance in limiting the right of access where there was no tradition of openness. Brennan, he said, ignored "a long history" of ex-

[123]Globe Newspaper Co. v. Superior Court, 423 N.E.2d 773, 781 (1981).
[124]457 U.S. at 605–06.
[125]*Id.* at 605 n.13 (emphasis in original).

clusion of the public from trials involving rape, especially when minors were involved. The Court had read *Richmond Newspapers* "as spelling out a First Amendment right of access to all aspects of all criminal trials under all circumstances," a reading Burger called "plainly incorrect."[126]

The Court in *Globe* also offered some guidance in how courts should weigh competing concerns. For a judge to close a courtroom without violating the First Amendment, the Court ruled, required the application of the strict scrutiny test: The judge must show that denial of access was required by "a compelling governmental interest" and that the remedy (closure) was "narrowly tailored" to serve that interest.[127]

In *Globe,* the Court found the state's interest in protecting minor victims of sexual offenses from further trauma and embarrassment a compelling governmental interest, but found that the mandatory closure statute was not narrowly tailored. Case-by-case evaluation was necessary because "it is clear that the circumstances of the particular case may affect the significance of the interest" of the government in closing the proceeding.[128]

Thus, while *Globe* gave lower courts some guidance in how to apply the *Richmond Newspapers* test, it raised as many questions as it answered. Brennan's treatment of the history prong was particularly confusing; it was not clear whether he had meant to say that *all* criminal trials must be open, to declare the history prong irrelevant, or merely to downplay the history prong because it did not suit the outcome he desired in this particular case.

His failure to explain the status of the history prong also made it difficult to know how the *Globe* case might be extended beyond criminal trials. Chief Justice Burger had hinted in *Richmond Newspapers* that civil trials would be presumptively open as well, given his historical analysis. "Whether the public has a right to attend trials of civil cases is a question not raised by this case," he wrote in a footnote, "but we note that historically both civil and criminal trials have been presumptively open."[129] Whether the same presumption would lie given Brennan's emphasis on the structural role in *Globe* was less clear.

The Court heard several more press access cases after *Globe*, but did little to dispel the confusion that remained. In *Press-Enterprise*

[126]*Id.* at 613 (Burger, C.J., dissenting).
[127]*Id.* at 606–07.
[128]*Id.* at 607–08.
[129]448 U.S. at 581 n.17.

Co. v. Superior Court[130] (known as *Press-Enterprise I*), the Court found a First Amendment right of access to pretrial jury selection proceedings in a criminal case, using both the historical prong and the structural prong. In *Waller v. Georgia*,[131] the Court mixed its *Richmond Newspapers* doctrine into what was essentially a Sixth Amendment claim. The Court found that the defendant's Sixth Amendment right to a fair trial had been violated when a pretrial suppression hearing was closed against his wishes. The Court also hinted, although it did not rule, that the public had a First Amendment right to attend the hearing.[132]

Two years later, in *Press-Enterprise Co. v. Superior Court* (*Press-Enterprise II*),[133] the Court all but overruled its decision in *Gannett* when it held that the public has a "qualified" First Amendment right of access to preliminary hearings in criminal cases if the history and structural prongs were satisfied. That right may be restricted in order to protect the defendant's Sixth Amendment rights, but only if the closure passed the *Globe* strict scrutiny test.[134] In 1993, the Supreme Court reaffirmed its decision in *Press-Enterprise II* when it overturned a law in Puerto Rico that allowed closed preliminary hearings at the request of the defendant.[135]

Richmond Newspapers and its progeny have thus set forth a doctrine on courtroom access that, at a minimum, recognizes a First Amendment right of access to some judicial proceedings based on two primary sources: (1) a history of openness and (2) the structural role of access, through a finding that public access plays a significant positive role in the functioning of the particular proceeding in question.[136] The right is not absolute and must be weighed against countervailing interests, which may include the defendant's Sixth Amendment right to a fair trial. In balancing these interests, courts must apply a strict scrutiny standard: the interest must be compelling and the closure must be narrowly tailored to serve that interest.

---

[130]464 U.S. 501 (1984).

[131]467 U.S. 39 (1984).

[132]*See id.* at 46–47 (listing advantages of open trials that benefit the public at large).

[133]478 U.S. 1 (1986).

[134]In *Globe*, the Court had ruled that the Court had correctly closed the courtroom based on a "reasonable probability of prejudice" to the defendant. 443 U.S. at 392–93. In *Press-Enterprise II*, the Court required a finding of "a substantial probability that the defendant's right to a fair trial" would be violated and that reasonable alternatives to closure would fail to adequately protect that right. 478 U.S. at 14.

[135]El Vocero de Puerto Rico v. Puerto Rico, 508 U.S. 147 (1993).

[136]*Press-Enterprise II*, 478 U.S. at 8–10.

The Legacy of Richmond Newspapers

The *Richmond Newspapers* test, as refined by *Globe* and the *Press-Enterprise* cases, has proved confusing to the lower courts. The Court's ambiguity about the relative importance of the two prongs and its lack of guidance regarding the extent of the right or its application to proceedings beyond criminal trials has led to an inconsistent application of the doctrine.

Most courts have attempted to apply the *Richmond Newspapers* two-pronged test, although the details of the application vary. Some courts have relied on the historical tradition of openness alluded to by Burger in *Richmond Newspapers* to expand the constitutional right of access to civil trials.[137] In analyzing the historical tradition of specific proceedings, some have drawn analogies with established proceedings[138] or have examined the history, however short, of the specific proceeding at issue.[139] In areas where public access has clearly not been a tradition in American law, such as family court proceedings[140] or grand juries,[141] courts have been reluctant to find a presumptive right of access under the First Amendment.

Other courts have taken their cue from Brennan's *Globe* reasoning and discounted the importance of a tradition of openness in favor of an examination of the structural value of access. In *United States v. Chagra*, the United States Court of Appeals for the Fifth Circuit

---

[137]*See, e.g.*, Publicker Indus. v. Cohen, 733 F.2d 1059 (3d. Cir. 1984) (finding a right of access to motions hearings in corporate litigation based on history of openness of civil proceedings); Brown & Williamson Tobacco Corp. v. Federal Trade Commission, 710 F.2d 1165 (6th Cir. 1983) (suit challenging FTC's testing methodology).

[138]*See, e.g*, First Amendment Coalition v. Judicial Inquiry & Review Bd., 784 F.2d 467, 484–85 (3d Cir. 1986) (Adams, J., concurring in part and dissenting in part) (calling for an analogy between judicial disciplinary proceedings and judicial impeachment hearings, which had historically been open); Society of Professional Journalists v. Secretary of Labor, 616 F. Supp. 569 (D. Utah 1985) (analogizing administrative fact-finding proceedings to civil trials, which enjoyed long history of openness), *appeal dismissed and judgement below vacated and remanded as moot,* 832 F.2d 1180 (10th Cir 1987).

[139]*See, e.g., First Amendment Coalition,* 784 F.2d at 472 (extent of access right must be guided by "unique history and function" of 14-year-old Judicial Review Board).

[140]*See, e.g.*, San Bernardino Co. Dept. of Public Soc. Services v. Superior Court, 232 Cal. App. 3d 188 (Cal. Ct. App. 1991) (First Amendment right of access does not extend to juvenile dependency proceedings, based in part on history of closed proceedings).

[141]*See, e.g.*, In re Donovan, 801 F.2d 409 (D.C. Cir. 1986) (per curiam) (no First Amendment right of access to grand jury materials in criminal investigation of labor secretary due to long tradition of grand jury secrecy and need for secrecy for proper functioning of grand juries).

found that access to bail reduction hearings "should not be foreclosed" just because the hearings lacked the history of openness relied on in *Richmond Newspapers*.[142] Because bail reduction hearings required decisions "that attract significant public interest, and invite legitimate and healthy public scrutiny," the same societal interests at stake in *Richmond Newspapers,* they mandated a First Amendment right of access.[143] Another court applied *Richmond Newspapers* to find a First Amendment right of access to presidential press conferences, despite a comparatively short history of access "going back through several past Administrations."[144]

Other courts have extended the reasoning of *Richmond Newspapers* to claims of a right of access to court documents, with a wide range of outcomes. The Ninth Circuit relied in part on a history of access to find a First Amendment right of access to pretrial documents in general.[145] The Eleventh Circuit, on the other hand, recently ruled that access to discovery materials did not rise to the level of a constitutional right and was properly left to the discretion of the trial court.[146]

Even in the context of a criminal trial, where the structural interest is arguably stronger, courts have denied access. In *United States v. McVeigh*,[147] for example, the Tenth Circuit affirmed the district court's sealing of documents from the Oklahoma City bombing trial by applying the two-prong test after assuming, *arguendo*, that there was some First Amendment right of access to the documents. The court ruled that the trial judge's findings of a likelihood of prejudicial publicity satisfied the requirement for closure.[148]

The courts have been similarly divided in cases involving administrative proceedings. The two-pronged test has been used to deny ac-

[142]701 F.2d 354, 363 (5th Cir. 1983).

[143]*Id. See also* Newman v Graddick, 696 F.2d 796 (11th Cir. 1983) (public access to hearings in class action suit over prison overcrowding was beneficial and stemmed from "legitimate interest"); In re Consumers Power Co. Sec. Litig., 109 F.R.D. 45, 53–54 (E.D. Mich. 1985) ("[I]t is appropriate for courts to go beyond the historical analysis ... and to consider ... what information will '[make] a positive contribution to the process of self-governance.'").

[144]Cable News Network v. American Broad. Cos., 518 F. Supp. 1238, 1244 (N.D. Ga. 1981) (calling short history of pool coverage an "enduring and vital tradition of public entree").

[145]Associated Press v. United States Dist. Court, 705 F.2d 1143, 1145 (9th Cir. 1983). *See also* United States v. Miller, 579 F. Supp. 862 (S.D. Fla. 1984) (recognizing a right of access to affidavit tapes in criminal case).

[146]Chicago Tribune Co. v. Bridgestone/Firestone, Inc., 263 F.3d 1304, 1310 (11th Cir. 2001).

[147]119 F.3d 806 (10th Cir. 1997).

[148]*Id.* at 815.

cess to involuntary commitment hearings[149] and judicial and medical disciplinary proceedings.[150] At the same time, courts have found a First Amendment right of access under the *Richmond Times* test for unemployment benefits hearings,[151] and in *Society of Professional Journalists v. Secretary of Labor*, a federal district court found a First Amendment right of access to the administrative fact-finding hearings of the federal Mine Safety and Health Administration.[152] There was little historical tradition to go by, the court found, given that administrative hearings of this type were of relatively recent origin. Still, the hearing at issue was analogous to a civil trial, the court ruled. Furthermore, "to the extent that there is a [general] tradition of holding this type of hearing, there is a tradition that the hearings have been open to the public," despite the fact that the MSHA itself had almost always closed its hearings to the public.[153]

Thus, the *Richmond Newspapers* test has been extended in widely varying ways to new types of judicial proceedings, administrative proceedings, court documents and even presidential press conferences. In many cases, the history prong could be used either to limit or expand access, depending on whether the court examines the tradition of openness for the particular proceeding (as in MSHA hearings), for similar proceedings (as in administrative fact-finding hearings), or for general types of proceedings (as with civil trials). The structural prong, because its basis is "theoretically endless," fails to give much guidance to courts in deciding how the public good is best served in a particular case, so courts often resort to an *ad hoc* balancing of interests in making access decisions.

Whether a First Amendment right of access will be found in INS proceedings such as those at issue in Michigan and New Jersey or in the military tribunals of Guantanamo Bay, therefore, depends on how a judge may weigh a number of indeterminate factors, and the

---

[149]*See, e.g.*, Tribune Co. v. D.M.L., 566 So.2d 1333 (Fla. Dist. Ct. App. 1990) (public policy of protecting confidentiality of patients was sufficient to overcome any right of public access to proceeding).

[150]*See, e.g.*, Johnson Newspaper Corp. v. Melino, 564 N.E.2d 1046 (N.Y. 1990) (dentist's disciplinary proceeding did not meet either criterion of two-prong test for public right of access); First Amendment Coalition v. Judicial Inquiry & Review Bd., 784 F.2d 467 (3d Cir. 1986) (finding an insufficient showing of need for public access to judicial misconduct hearings).

[151]*See, e.g.*, Herald Co. v. Weisenberg, 455 N.Y.S.2d 413, *aff'd*, 59 N.Y.2d 378 (N.Y. Sup. Ct. 1982) (hearing was presumptively open and administrative law judge did not have authority to close hearing without a finding of sufficient need for closure).

[152]616 F. Supp. 569, 575 (D. Utah 1985).

[153]*Id.*

outcome in neither situation is clear. Instead of providing a "value proposition of sufficient generality and thrust"[154] to be largely outcome-determinative, today's courtroom access doctrine offers little principled guidance to the judges who must decide these issues. At the same time, the political pressures on those judges are intense. Predicting how the *Richmond Newspapers* test would apply in these cases would be a difficult task even in the best of times. In pathological times, it is impossible.

COURTROOM ACCESS FROM A PATHOLOGICAL PERSPECTIVE

Constructing a doctrine of courtroom access that would lend greater predictability to the analysis would be beneficial for a number of reasons. First, as Blasi pointed out, clarity and stability give legal principles moral force:

> Only relatively stable principles are likely to be perceived by divergent political factions as potentially working to their advantage in the long run. Only relatively stable principles are likely to be viewed as worthy of a certain respect simply on account of their capacity to endure.[155]

Second, a rule that limits a judge's discretion in deciding questions of core values can better preserve those values during times of stress when pressures may affect proper decision making. Courtroom access doctrine from the pathological perspective, therefore, must be clear, stable and robust—a rule targeted for the worst of times.

Before any attempt is made to fashion such a rule, however, a threshold question must be answered: Is courtroom access a proper subject for the pathological perspective? Blasi contended that, in order to preserve the integrity of the constitutional regime during times of pathology, First Amendment doctrine must address itself to a limited number of core values. In his article, Blasi discussed courtroom access as part of the broader issue of the public's right to know, a concept he found too expansive and prone to *ad hoc* balancing to be reducible to a simple and clear rule as required by the pathological perspective. Because the circumstances in which a right to know may be invoked are so variable—access to prisons, courtrooms and government documents—"one despairs of developing a set of stable, concise principles to govern adjudication regarding the right to know."[156]

---

[154]Blasi, *supra* note 3, at 473.
[155]*Id.* at 454.
[156]*Id.* at 490.

Blasi may be correct that a general right to know is too broad and undefined to be considered a core value, at least given the Court's general reluctance to acknowledge such a right beyond certain parameters. But *Richmond Newspapers* and its progeny show that the Court did regard one subset of the public's right to know as an important and constitutionally protected right: access to trials. Courtroom access is a core First Amendment value for the reasons Burger and Brennan outlined in *Richmond Newspapers*. Therefore, it needs to be preserved and protected by a robust doctrine that will withstand the pressures of pathological times.

The Court's *Richmond Newspapers* test, it is clear, fails under the pathological perspective. Like most First Amendment doctrines Blasi criticized as over-complex and over-refined, the law of courtroom access lacks the simplicity of analysis and clarity of description that Blasi would require. The Court's courtroom access doctrine fails from a pathological perspective because it does not provide clear guidance based on fundamental principles that would guide lower courts in times both good and bad.

Blasi's formulation of First Amendment doctrine from the pathological perspective is focused primarily on instrumental concerns; that is, the formulation of doctrine so that "abstract conceptions and priority judgments"[157] are translated into working tools that will be effective during times of stress. The first step in formulating doctrine is to pare away all but the core values worth preserving. The pathological perspective, Blasi said, requires a "lean" First Amendment, stripped to the essentials:

> In pathological periods, courts need to present the forces of repression with strict, immutable legal constraints. That kind of implacable judicial posture is easier to assume when the basic reach of the First Amendment is modest and compatible with widely shared intuitions regarding the natural ambit of the commitment to expressive liberty.[158]

Narrowly drawn First Amendment rights can be protected by doctrine that is "simple, informed by tradition, and dominated by principles."[159] Therefore, the first step in fashioning a doctrine of courtroom access under the pathological perspective is to limit its ambit.

For courtroom access, this can be done by limiting the doctrine so that it applies only to judicial proceedings. Because a doctrine tar-

[157] *Id.* at 466.
[158] *Id.* at 478.
[159] *Id.* at 479.

geted for pathological times must "speak to persons who are neither First Amendment specialists nor devotees,"[160] the definition of a "judicial proceeding" can be determined by its generally accepted meaning: any procedure involving the formal examination of a matter before a tribunal in a civil or criminal cause in order to determine the matter.[161] Thus, both criminal and civil trials would fall under the doctrine, as would related hearings before, during or after a trial that go toward the determination of the matter at hand. It would also include quasi-judicial and administrative proceedings, as long as they fit within the definition (informal fact-finding hearings, for instance, would not be included). Anything based on a more general principle of the public's right to know—presidential press conferences, government documents, discovery materials—would fall outside the scope of the rule.

This definition both narrows and enlarges courtroom access doctrine from its current state. While government documents, press conferences and the like are beyond its scope, the rule expands the range of proceedings that fall within the doctrine by eliminating the need for the two-pronged test of *Richmond Newspapers*. Rather than each court making its own determination of a particular proceeding's tradition of openness and its structural/functional value, the new rule is based on a more general proposition that access to *all* judicial proceedings is protected under the First Amendment.

This rule makes sense under the pathological perspective because it simplifies the analysis while keeping an eye to traditional commitments and the core values at stake. As Chief Justice Burger pointed out in *Richmond Newspapers*, both criminal and civil proceedings have a long history of openness in the United States. This history is important, but only as it supports the functional and structural view of the role of access to those proceedings. Historical tradition alone cannot be dispositive; too many cherished First Amendment principles are relatively new and too many long-held principles (slavery, the disenfranchisement of women) have been discarded to rely exclusively on history for what is valuable. The individual analysis of history required by the *Richmond Newspapers* test is unnecessary and frequently misguided: The examination of the "history of openness" on the part of the Mine Safety and Health Administration in *Society*

[160] *Id.* at 471.

[161] *See* MERRIAM-WEBSTER'S COLLEGIATE DICTIONARY (10th ed.) at 1255 (definition of "trial").

of Professional Journalists proves the barrenness of this level of analysis.[162]

Rather than focusing on the historical tradition of openness, then, courtroom access from a pathological perspective takes a fundamentally structuralist approach, based on the idea that *all* judicial proceedings reveal vital information about how the government is doing its job and therefore must be open. Justice Harry Blackmun, in his dissent in *Gannett v. DePasquale,* quoted a list created by Jeremy Bentham of the benefits of open proceedings that is instructive. First, he said, public trials "protect against judicial, prosecutorial and police abuse." They "provide a means for citizens to obtain information about the criminal justice system and the performance of public officials." Third, they "safeguard the integrity of the courts." Finally, "publicity is essential to the preservation of public confidence in the rule of law and in the operation of the courts."[163]

While Blackmun's *Gannett* dissent was based on the Sixth Amendment, his list is a structuralist argument for a First Amendment right of trial access. Courtroom access has as its core purpose the oversight of the government by the citizenry. By facilitating information gathering, public access to judicial proceedings allows the public to act as a check on the government and educates the public about the justice system so citizens can exercise their sovereign powers over its administration. Furthermore, these benefits and the oversight role they encompass apply to *any* judicial proceeding, because the citizenry must oversee the administration of justice in *all* contexts, whether criminal or civil, in a courtroom or in an administrative proceeding.

Thus the pathological perspective takes as its starting point the view that it is almost always beneficial to have judicial proceedings open to the public and the press, and, therefore, that all such proceedings are presumptively open. This change would take away the ability of judges to engage in *ad hoc* decision making and would bring about a higher level of certainty regarding courtroom access. After all, the Court has said, "A trial is a public event. What transpires in the courtroom is public property."[164]

Once a First Amendment value is stripped to its core, the pathological perspective requires that the doctrine be expressed as a "principle;" that is, as a "value proposition of sufficient generality and

---

[162]*See supra* notes 152–53 and accompanying text.

[163]443 U.S. 368, 448 (1979) (Blackmun, J., dissenting), *quoting* Jeremy Bentham, A TREATISE ON JUDICIAL EVIDENCE 67 (1825).

[164]Craig v. Harney, 331 U.S. 367, 374 (1947).

thrust"[165] that its application will be dispositive in most cases. The pathological perspective-derived principle of courtroom access might be summarized as, "Judicial proceedings operate under a strong presumption of openness." As the operating principle for courtroom access, this statement has both the simplicity of analysis and the clarity of description that Blasi advocated. Like the prohibition against prior restraints, this principle has "thrust"—acceptance or rejection of the proposition will largely determine how a case is resolved. Judges, lawyers, litigants, reporters and the public at large can understand what rule will operate.

Instead of the *Richmond Newspapers* two-pronged test, which allows for significant flexibility of analysis, courtroom access under the pathological perspective would limit a trial judge's discretion. Rather than performing an exacting analysis of the type of proceeding at issue and its historical tradition of openness, the judge would proceed under the assumption that the proceeding will be open to all. The public and the press would be relieved of the burden of filing costly motions to force access; instead, the burden would fall to the party seeking closure.

Closure may be warranted in some cases; after all, the principle of courtroom access, even under the pathological perspective, is not absolute. As with the presumption against prior restraints, the presumption for openness can be overcome. In this aspect, current courtroom access doctrine has it right: The presumption can be overcome only by showing a compelling countervailing interest and by narrowly tailoring closure to serve that interest. What constitutes a compelling interest would not change; it may include the defendant's right to a fair trial or other reasons that necessitate secrecy, such as the need for confidentiality in grand jury proceedings.

National security, for example, may be considered a compelling interest for purposes of the strict scrutiny test under the pathological perspective, as it is under traditional First Amendment analysis.[166] Still, even such a compelling interest as national security must be considered on a case-by-case basis. The court must make a finding that the interest is, indeed, compelling and that the proposed closure is narrowly tailored and that no less restrictive alternative exists. Employing this strict scrutiny test is acceptable under the pathological perspective because, even though strict scrutiny lacks the sim-

[165]Blasi, *supra* note 3, at 473.

[166]*See, e.g.*, Snepp v. United States, 444 U.S. 507, 510 (1980) (government has a compelling interest in protecting the secrecy of information important to national security).

plicity of broader principles, it is a well-established standard familiar to judges that average citizens can understand. Furthermore, it allows for the rare case in which the public interest truly is served by closure.

What would this new doctrine look like? In practice, courtroom access under the pathological perspective may look similar to the *Richmond Newspapers* test. After all, both tests allow for countervailing interests to overcome the principle of openness. What the pathological perspective principle offers that the current two-pronged test does not is a *fixed baseline* for analysis of the countervailing interests. Under the pathological perspective, judges start their analysis from a presumption of openness.

The Haddad case provides an example of the differences. In that case, District Court Judge Nancy G. Edmunds ruled in April 2002 that the blanket closure by the attorney general of INS hearings of "special interest" did not serve a compelling interest and was therefore unconstitutional.[167] A judge applying courtroom access doctrine under the pathological perspective may have made an identical ruling.

As a preliminary matter, however, Judge Edmunds was required to examine a fundamental threshold issue: "whether the First Amendment of the United States Constitution confers upon the Newspaper Plaintiffs a right of access to [INS deportation] proceedings."[168] The judge applied the analysis laid out in *Richmond Newspapers* and its progeny and found a presumptive right of access for the proceedings based on her finding of a historical tradition of openness for deportation proceedings, the procedural importance of access to such proceedings and the existence of specific INS regulations that mandated a presumption of openness for such proceedings.[169] Under the pathological perspective, however, the deportation proceedings would have been presumptively open without the need for the detailed analysis that Judge Edmunds was required to perform. Thus the pathological principle, by setting a strong presumption of openness for all types of judicial proceedings, allows for closure in the rare instance when it is needed while "plac[ing] a premium on confining the range of discretion left to future decisionmakers who will be called upon the make judgments when pathological pressures are most intense."[170]

---

[167]Detroit Free Press v. Ashcroft, 195 F. Supp. 2d 937 (E.D. Mich. 2002).
[168]*Id.* at 942.
[169]Id. at 942–47.
[170]Blasi, *supra* note 3, at 474.

CONCLUSIONS

To be successful under the pathological perspective, a First Amendment doctrine should be streamlined enough that it can be framed in terms of a simple precept. Jeremy Bentham's adage "Publicity is the soul of justice" may be an apt description for the courtroom access doctrine under the pathological perspective.[171] Like other "well-worn homilies" that describe our free speech tradition,[172] this precept has the "kind of emotional force that may be most effective in reversing or containing the dangerous attitude shifts that take place in pathological periods."[173]

A pathological perspective doctrine of courtroom access would rest on a strong presumption of openness for all judicial proceedings, while allowing narrowly tailored closure if necessary to protect compelling countervailing interests. Definitional problems would no doubt remain, but this rule speaks with a clarity and simplicity that may prevent some violations of the right of public access by rhetorical force alone. It would force discipline on what otherwise is a largely *ad hoc* decision making process and would signal to the public that public trials are the constitutional norm. Indeed, the wide acceptance of a narrow but robust rule against courtroom closures might have prevented the recent actions of the president and the attorney general by putting the constitutional onus on those who would take away the right of access.

The right of access to judicial proceedings is a core constitutional value that is too important to leave to the discretion of trial judges, a fact that has been made clear by the developments of recent months. The Supreme Court has failed to provide clear guidance to lower courts for protecting the public's right of access, but the Court can fix that error by making a strong declaration that *all* judicial proceedings should be open to the public absent a compelling reason for closure.

Judge Edmunds ruled in favor of public access in the INS proceedings, and a court may make a similar ruling with regard to military tribunals. This result would not obviate the need for changes in courtroom access doctrine, however. A new rule is needed because, regardless of the outcome in a particular case, the circumstantial analysis required by existing doctrine is the sort of variable decision making that the pathological perspective is designed to avoid.

---

[171]1 JEREMY BENTHAM, RATIONALE OF JUDICIAL EVIDENCE 524 (1827), *quoted in* Richmond Newspapers, Inc. v. Virginia, 448 U.S. 555, 569 (1980).

[172]*See supra*, note 49 and accompanying text.

[173]Blasi, *supra* note 3, at 472.

For Product Safety Concerns and Information please contact our EU representative GPSR@taylorandfrancis.com
Taylor & Francis Verlag GmbH, Kaufingerstraße 24, 80331 München, Germany

www.ingramcontent.com/pod-product-compliance
Ingram Content Group UK Ltd.
Pitfield, Milton Keynes, MK11 3LW, UK
UKHW050756180926
475701UK00007B/1076
9780805896343